# INSPIRE!!!

## ASPIRE FOR ASSERTIVENESS.....

# By

# Vincent Happy Mnisi

Edited by Mandisa Mundwarara

This book is dedicated to my family and friends...

# Contents

# Chapter 1: Intro

Good day to you, may your life be at peace with it's self, and may it overflow with peace, love and pure awesomeness today and everyday of your life...By Vincent Happy Mnisi. May the sun bring you new energy by day, May the moon softly restore you by night, May the rain wash away your worries, May the breeze blow new strength into your being, May you walk gently through the world and know it's beauty all the days of your life...An Apache Blessing. God created humankind and gave them their rights to live their lives. With that right God gave mankind the power of discretion, which is the power to choose their own course of action. Without discretion, life is meaningless...By Vincent Happy Mnisi

Mankind was given the freedom to choose from many alternatives that surrounds them. Their chooses will determine who they are in life. Mankind's greatest privilege is to enjoy the presence of God in their chosen religion, as humankind was created different with vast cultural differences and values we all devised a way to pray to God hence there are so many Religions on earth... By Vincent Happy Mnisi. If you're reading this then I hope something good happens to you today....By Codeblack and Vincent Happy Mnisi. Dear whoever is reading this: I hope you have a reason to smile today....By Basiden Live. Don't worry everything is going to be amazing...By Rev Run.

Go forward in life with a twinkle in your eye and a smile on your face, but with great and strong purpose in your heart...By Gordon. B. Hinkley. Your purpose in life, you should have one or several which can be changed from time to time. One purpose everybody should have is to making the world a better place. Everybody's life is full of obstacles. Obstacles are lessons and once you learn to live a life with purpose in your heart; you are living a life of purpose...By Vincent Happy Mnisi. Starting today, I need to forget what's gone appreciate what still remains, and look forward to what's coming next...Unknown.

You don't need permission to follow your dreams, you are the leader in your life and are worthy of all the joy in the world. Ask yourself what is really important, and then have the wisdom and courage to build your life around your answer...By Energy Therapy. Having a rough morning? Place your hand over your heart. Feel that? That's called purpose. You are alive for a reason; don't give up...By BeginWithYes. Have the courage to be yourself...By Panache Desai. At this stage in my life, if it doesn't 1) make me happy? 2)make me better? 3)Make me money?. I don't make time for it...By Baisden Live...

There are far, far better things ahead than any we leave behind...By C.S.Lewis. You must find the place inside yourself where nothing is impossible...By Deepak Chopra. If your dreams don't scare you, they aren't big enough...By Baisden Live. It's time, time to stop living your life because of what other people expect. Time to walk your own path and follow your own dreams. Time to let go of fear and allow your heart to lead you...By Kate Spencer.

I know what I want. I can say No when I need to and I can say Yes When I need to. I have the confidence to say what I mean...By Lynda Fields. It's finally time to drop those negative thoughts about yourself; they are only getting in your way. Never mind whatever it is, that you think you can't do...concentrate instead on what you can do...By Lynda Field Life Coach. "Always speak the truth even if your voice shakes...Anonymous. You spend your whole life looking for that one person to make you happy and complete never realising that one person is YOU!!!...By GrowingBolder.com. The ability to speak several languages is an asset, but the ability to keep your mouth shut in any language is priceless...By Music For Deep. Live simply, Be grateful. Love more. Dream Big, Laugh Lots and have Faith...By Power of Positivity.comMy advice is never to never do tomorrow what you can do today. Procrastination is the thief of time...By Charles Dickens. I have too many flaws to be perfect. But I have too many blessings to be ungrateful...By Shashicka Tyre-Hill.

Be Happy; Be Bright; Be You! The distance between your dreams and reality is called Action...By Wisdom Starting today, I need to forget what's gone, appreciate what still remains and look forward to what's coming next...Unknown. Don't start your day with the broken pieces of yesterday. Every day is a fresh start. Each day is a new beginning. Every morning we wake up is the first day of our new Life!!!....By IBelieve,com. Happiness is the bright level of success...By KushandWizdom.Codeblacklife.

Be of good cheer, it's still a fabulous year!...By Kenni Gambo. But the path of the righteous is like the light of Dawn, which shines Brighter and Brighter until full Day....Some days I wonder how, I've held on this long, but I'm reminded that with struggle comes strength...Don't give up...Keep going....By Rato KasiSoul Molaba. Healing doesn't mean the damage never existed, it means the damage no longer controls our lives...Indian Proverbs. Optimism is the one quality more associated with success and happiness than any other...By Brain Tracy. Success is no accident. It is hard work, perseverance, learning, studying, sacrifice and most of all love of what you are doing or learning to do...By Pele. Sometimes all you need is a hundred million dollars...By Sue Fitzmaurice.

Take nothing for granted everyday is a blessing, embrace the struggles. Let it make you stronger for success. Your blessings are on the way the way!...By Tony Gaskins. Nothing ever goes away until it teaches us what we need to know...By Pema Chodron. You are not born a winner and your are not born a loser. You are born a chooser...By Incredible Joy. Decide once and for all to have an extraordinary life...By Prosperity Fairy. Whatever you believe with conviction becomes reality...By Brain Tracy. Every morning start a new page in your story. Make it great one today...By Doe Zantamata. Meditate. Contemplate. Create. Breathe. Repeat...By Lisa Renee Wilson. Creative people: 1) Easily bored. 2) Risk takers. 3) Colour outside the lines. 4) Think with their hearts. 5) Make lots of mistakes 6) Hate the rules. 7) Work Independently 8) Change their minds a lot. 9) Have a reputation for eccentricity 10) Dream big....Unknown. If you have good thoughts they will shine out of your face like sunbeam and you will always look lovely...By Wisdom Sayings.

Once you connect with yourself it is impossible to be lonely or desperate...By Bryant McGill. It's never too late to start doing the right thing. Start now. Forgive, love, start again. Whatever it is you need to do, just do it...By Manna Expresson-line.

Revive your light manifest your dreams, realise your worth...By Brain Tracy. If you expect the world to be fair with you because you are fair, with you because you are fair, you're fooling yourself. That's like expecting the lions not to eat you because you don't eat him...By Baisden Live. The most important thing to realise is yourself worth. When you know your worth you set the standards for you...By Necole Stephens. Don't be pushed by your problems. Be led by your dreams...By Ralph Waldo Emerson.

If you want to be Happy you must become a happiness seeker. You have to think about happiness, look for happiness and believe with all your heart that you deserve happiness...By Bryant McGill. Happiness is knowing you are fabulous...know that you are Fabulous! And let happiness have her fabulous way today...By Kenni Gambo. A Great attitude becomes a great mood. A Great mood becomes a great day. A Great day becomes a great year, a great year becomes a great life...Unknown. Integrity is doing the right thing when nobody is watching...By Nurturing Life. Some creations take time. Give the seeds of your dreams time to take root and find their way into the world. It's OK to take out to nourish your soul world. It's OK to take time out to nourish your soul and let the universe work it's magic...By Laurel Bleadon Mattei. In the age of information. Ignorance is a choice...By World Truth TV.

Dear whoever is reading this, I hope you have a reason to smile today...By Lifefm and Vincent Happy Mnisi. Have a Good day, may your hearts overflow with peace, love and pure awesomeness today and enjoy the read get Inspired!!!...By Vincent Happy Mnisi. I hope you have some adventures this week. I hope you discover something new. I hope you discover something new. I hope you get to see some beautiful things. And I hope you fell peace all the way through...By S.C. Lousie. Confidence is nothing more than believing in yourself, is about doing the things you once didn't believe you could do...By Steve Aitchison.

# Chapter 2: Good Life!!!

"A good life is when you smile often, dream big, laugh a lot and realise how blessed you are for what you have. Let your dreams be bigger than your fears and your actions louder than your words"...By We Are Humanity. Enjoy your life! Life is for us to live the best of what we best at, so discover what you are good at and share it with the world and make a mint...By Vincent Happy Mnisi.

"Learn to enjoy every minute of your life, be happy now don't wait for something outside of yourself to make you happy in the future. Think how really precious is the time you have to spend, whether it's at work or with your family. Every minute should be enjoyed and savoured"...By Earl Nightingale. Life is what we make it, always has been, always will be...By Grandma Moses. Promise yourself to be strong that nothing can disturb your peace of mind. Look at the sunny side of everything and make your optimism come true. Think only of the best, work only for the best and expect only the best. Forget the mistakes of the past and press on to the greater achievements of the future. Give so much time to the improvement of yourself that you have no time to criticise others. Live in faith that the whole world is on your side for as long as you are true to the best that is in you...By Christian.D. Larson.

Life is what you make out of what you can get from it, so do the best you can to enjoy it while you still can enjoy your life...By Vincent Happy Mnisi. Life is full of up's and down's, you just got to learn to adjust to them accordingly but it's best to learn from your down's in order for you to try and avoid them and also learn how to make the up's last longer than the last time...by Vincent Happy Mnisi. Surround yourself with the dreamers and the doers, the believers and thinkers, but most of all; surround yourself with those who see greatness within you, even when you don't see it yourself. There is no need to be jealous of others. What's for you is for you, and what they have wouldn't fit you anyway. Be thankful for all you have and know that all you desire is on the way... By Tony Gaskin.

When you believe in your purpose, you can work through obstacles, overcome disappointments, and endure hardship...By Billy Cox. Start where you are and use what you have and do what you can with all you have The purpose of our lives is to be happy...By Vincent Happy Mnisi. Just Do It...Nike. "You gotta do what you have to do, before you can do what you want to do. It's called priorities. I cannot do all the good that the world needs. But the world needs all the good that I can do"...By Jana Stanfield. Do not boast about tomorrow, for you do not know what a day may bring forth, let another man praise you and not your own mouth...Proverbs 27 v 1&2

You draw to you the people and events who resonate with the energy you are radiating. You attract what you are! So be your best. The best feeling in the world is knowing your presence and absence both mean something to someone. Always also keep reminding yourself that some people have been raised differently from your upbringing. Most of the important things in the world have been accomplished by people who have kept trying when there seemed to be no help at all. 97% of the people who quit too soon are employed by the 3% that never gave up...Patience is a virtue for sure, dreams are possible, aspirations are attainable. You just have to keep focused on your end goal...By Vincent Happy Mnisi. Never ever give up on your ambitions, there is always a way. Learn from yesterday, live for today and hope and pray for a better tomorrow...By Vincent Happy Mnisi. When you feel like quitting think about why you started. Follow your passion to find your purpose...By Sue Krebs.

Sometimes life doesn't want to give you something you want, not because you don't deserve it, but because you deserve more...By Killian Bukutu. Live your life by God's principle and not by people's opinions...By Rehabtime. Integrity is doing the right thing when no one is watching. Strength is when you have so much to cry for, but you choose to smile instead...By Inspirational Quotes. When we read we are able to travel to many places, meet many people and understand the world...By Nelson Rolihlahla Mandela.

Try not to feel jealous about things, or people or places. It's toxic, just keep living, you will find your happiness...Unknown. Life is a challenge rise to it...By livinglife2theful. When I believe in myself I can do anything...By Lyndafields.com. When you live, love and dream with an open heart, all things are possible. Bold living begins with bold expectations...By Joel Osteen. The happiness of your life depends upon the quality of your thoughts...By Marcus Aurelius. The choice to have a great attitude is something nobody or no circumstance can take from you...By Zig Ziglar.

If you want to succeed in your life remember this phrase: That the past does not equal the future. Because you failed yesterday, or all day today or a moment ago; or for the last six months; the last sixteen years; or the last fifty years of life doesn't mean anything. All that matters is what are you going to do right now?...By Anthony Robbins. The number one skill is not giving up...By Bryant McGill. This week, try releasing your past and fears. Have the intention to think bigger and take more action towards your dreams...By Brendon Burchard.

If you only knew the real power of your thoughts you would be very careful not to engage in negativity, train your mind and turn to the positive at all times...By Lyndafields.com. Train your mind to stop worrying about what you can't change and begin concentrating on what you can do instead...By Vincent Happy Mnisi. Your hardest times often lead to the greatest moments of your life. Keep the faith. It will be worth it in the end...By Killian Bukutu. Forget about all the reasons why something may not work. You only need to find one good reason why it will...By Killian Bukutu. I never lose...either I win or learn. Don't look back and wonder why things went wrong. Don't regret not doing more. It happened for a reason your better days are ahead of you...By Killian Bukutu.

I know that I have all the strength and confidence I need to overcome any challenge that life offers. I just need to remember this...By www.lyndafield.com. When you forgive you don't change the past, you change the future...If you want to succeed in your life, remember this phrase: That past does not equal the future. I am strong because I know weakness; I am beautiful because I am aware of my flaws; I am fearless because I learnt to recognise illusion from real; I am wise because I learnt from my mistakes; I am a lover because I have felt hate and I can laugh because I have known sadness. I am strong because I have been weak, I am fearless because I have been afraid, I am wise because I have been foolish, Hate no one, no matter how much they have wronged you. Live humbly, no matter how wealthy you become. Think positively, no matter how hard life is. Give much, even if you have been given little. Keep in touch with the ones who have forgotten you, and forgive who has wronged you, and do not stop praying for the best for those you love and hate...By Vincent Happy Mnisi

"Your time is limited, so don't waste it living someone else's life. Don't be trapped by dogma-which is living with the results of other peoples thinking. Don't let the noise of others opinions drown out your inner voice. And most important, have the courage to follow your heart and intuition"...by Steve Jobs. Keep your past your history and your future a mystery and treat the present like a gift...By Vincent Happy Mnisi.

My son, keep your father's command, and don't forsake the law of your mother, Bind them continually upon you tie them around your neck, when you roam, they will lead you; and when you sleep, they will keep you and when you awake, they will speak with you. For the commandment is a lamp and the law a light, reproofs of instruction are the way of life...Proverbs 6 v 20 to 23. Everybody has something special in them, but sometimes it may take someone else to help you realise it. When you come out of the storm of problems, you won't be the same person that walked in the storm. That's what the storm is all about...By Haruki Murakami.

"Your light is seen, your heart is known, your soul is cherished by more people than you might never imagine. If you knew how many others have been touched in wonderful ways by you, you would be astonished. If you knew how many people feel so much for you, you would be shocked. You are far more wonderful than you think you are. Rest with that, rest easy with that, Breathe again, you doing fine. More than fine, Better than fine. You are doing great, so relax, and love yourself today"...By Neale Donald Walsch. The best way to predict the future is to create one yourself...By Sifiso Ntuli.

"A wise man never knows all only fools know everything"...African Proverb. "Pay attention to the ones who care, instead of trying to get attention of those who don't"...By Powerplug. "I am not perfect but nevertheless I am unique, kind, thoughtful, positive and doing the best I can"...By Lynda Field life coach.

If you are depressed you are living in the past, if you are anxious, you are living in the future. If you are at peace, you are living in the present". By Loa Tzu. "When I was young I thought that money was the most important thing in life, now that I am older I know that it is". By Oscar Wilde "When I was poor and I complained about inequality they said I was bitter, but now that I am rich and I complain about inequality they say I am a hypocrite. I am starting to think they don't want to talk about inequality"...by Russell Brand. Don't judge unless you know the story and even if you know the story who the fuck are you to pass judgement anyway. Sometimes God closes doors because it's time to move forward. he knows you won't move unless your circumstances force you. Trust me!..By Vincent Happy Mnisi.

What if? What if our religion was each other? If our practice was our life? If prayer was our words? What if the temple was the earth? If forests were our churches? If holy water, the rivers, lakes and oceans? What if meditation was our relationships? If wisdom was self-knowledge? If love was the centre of our being...a poem By Ganga White. Trust in God's perfect plan, even when it doesn't make no sense. Life has knocked me down a few times. It has shown me things I have never wanted to see. I have experienced sadness and failures. But one thing is for sure, I always get up! to face another day...Unknown.

I am in competition with no one. I have no desire to play the game of being better than anyone. I am simply trying to be better than the person I was yesterday. If you want to feel rich, just count the things you have that money can't buy. Fear does not prevent death. It prevents life...By Naguib Mahfouz. Because once you fear to attempting you will never succeed in anything, you must always believe that you are born to achieve and overcome everything that confronts you in life. Problems and hardship are testing your capabilities and abilities in coping with harsh realities in life...By Vincent Happy Mnisi. "Walking, I am listening to a deeper way, suddenly all my ancestors are behind me. Be still they say, watch and listen. You are the result of the love of thousands...that have come before you by Linda Hogan (1947) Native Indian American writer. Also believe that you are born for a purpose and that all your ancestors are backing you up...By Vincent Happy Mnisi.

Six ethics of life; Before you pray-believe; Before you speak-listen; Before you spend-Earn; Before you write-think; Before you quit-try; Before you die-live...By www.Auesomequotes4.com. Don't take for granted what it means to have 20/20 vision, "Believe with your eyes, not your ears!"...By Killian Bukutu.

There is a difference between knowing somebody and hearing about somebody. Just because you heard, doesn't mean you know them....By Trent Shelton. We are only fully alive when we're helping others....By Rick Warren. "Don't let the behaviour of others destroy your Inner peace"...By H.H. Dalai Lama. "If everyone is a product of this society, who will say the things that need to be said, and do the things that need to be done, without compromise? The truth will never start out popular in a world more concerned with marketability than righteousness. It will initially suffer ridicule and even violence yet ultimately it is undeniable. All of humanity is living in a dream world, but suffering real consequences" By Layrn Hill-Marley.

The most expensive thing in the world is trust, as it can take years to earn and just a matter of seconds to lose" By Tupac Pac Shakur. "Drop the idea of becoming someone, because you are already a masterpiece. You cannot be improved, you have only to come to it to know it and realise it...By Leizee Gurl.

Because all it takes is for you to discover your true calling and inner talent which will make your efforts unique and outstanding, everybody will want a piece of you and then you can charge them a fee for your time and efforts...By Vincent Happy Mnisi.

Even though sometimes you may want to break down and cry about the shit that you going through behind closed doors, the hard work you put seems to get nowhere and all the minor setbacks...but then you have to realise that this is part of life, so just suck it up, put a smile on your face, bite the bullet and keep moving! because nobody cares about your struggles and there is nobody who is going to keep trying to achieve your goals but you...By Vincent Happy Mnisi "You have enemies? Good, that means you have stood up for something in your life" By Winston Churchill. There is a difference between knowing somebody and hearing about somebody. Just because you heard, doesn't mean you know them....By Trent Shelton. We are only fully alive when we're helping others....By Rick Warren.

"Don't let the behaviour of others destroy your Inner peace"...By H.H. Dalai Lama. "Your background and circumstances may have influenced who you are, but you are responsible for who you become"...By Darren Hardy.

One good reason we should all pray at times, is because God can do more in a second than we can do ourselves in our lifetimes.... Never and don't rush on anything, when the time is right, it will happen for you. When God decides to use you, he will baffle the spectators as he does not make normal moves. When God moves in your life, no one will be able to deny his presence". By Tony. A. Gaskin jr. Always thank God in advance for the blessings you are about to receive, like every breath you breath...By Vincent Happy Mnisi. The words we speak can be used as weapons to hurt or destroy...or they can be used as medicine to heal a broken heart, the choice is ours so choose wisely...By David L. Hill.

When nobody else celebrates with you then learn to celebrate by yourself. When nobody else compliments you, then compliment yourself. It's not up to other people to keep you encouraged; it's up to you as encouragement should come from the inside. As there will be haters, there will be doubters, there will be non-believers, and then there will be you proving them wrong. Fake people are the worst people as they always appear to be happy when inside they are so jealous and hurting over someone's else life!, just as good as closet racist who smile to you face while in the inside they are cursing you to kingdom come!...By Vincent Happy Mnisi

Change of Address: From January 2015 onwards I will no longer be living on the corner of Depression and Doubt Street, The rent is too high, the space is too small and there's no room for my dreams to grow. My new place will be located over at Destiny and Belief Street...By Vincent Happy Mnisi. "The Man who views the world at fifty the same as he did when he was twenty has wasted thirty years of his life"...By Mohammed Ali. No matter how fucked up you think you think you are there will always be someone that loves you and still thinks you are amazing...By Vincent Happy Mnisi.

"Dam right I like the life I live, cause I went from negative to positive...By Biggie Smalls. "It's better to walk alone, than with a crowd going in the wrong direction" By Muhammad Gandhi.

"As we all have our part to play and it's not all up to God; you too have a role to play in enhancing your life"...By T.B Joshua Ministries. And why are you trying so hard to fit in, when you were born to stand out". Some people may think that you say inappropriate things at the wrong time, but just inform them that you are radically honest...By Vincent Happy Mnisi. Buy the truth and do not sell it, also wisdom and instruction and understanding. Proverbs 23v23. A person who feels appreciated will always do more than what is expected from them. "An entire sea of water can't sink a ship unless it get inside the ship. Similarly, the negativity of the world can't put you down unless you allow it to get inside you...Unknown. Emancipate yourself from mental slavery, none but ourselves can free our minds...By Bob Marley.

You! yes you! you reading this book, you are beautiful, talented, amazing and simply the best at being you! never forget that. You have to work towards your dreams, as dreams don't work unless you do! Be careful who you tell your secrets and be careful of who you pick as friends, most people pretend to listen, but are only gathering information to judge you with later and also spread rumours about you...By Vincent Happy Mnisi. When things aren't adding up in your life, start subtracting things and people out of your life that are always subtracting things and time out of your life...By Baisden live. Always cherish every moment and every person in your life because you never know when it will be the last time you see them...By Vincent Happy Mnisi

"Education is the key to everything that humankind may want or wish for in their life's"...By Nelson Mandela, "The secret of freedom lies in educating people, whereas the secret of tyranny is in keeping them ignorant... By Maximillien Robespierre." I am happy to be me, I may not be perfect but I am honest, loving and happy. I never try to be anything that I am not and I am not here to impress anyone else, I am me"...By Vincent Happy Mnisi. One lie is all it takes for a person to lose interest in you. Best thing to do is always be upfront, be real and tell the truth always. We don't meet people by accident. They are meant to cross our paths for a reason...By Vincent Happy Mnisi.

"When I was 5 years old my mother always told me that happiness was the key to life. When I went to school, they asked me what I wanted to be when I grew up, I wrote down Happy. They told me I didn't understand the assignment and I told them they didn't understand life"...By John Lennon.

Good parenting does not mean giving them a perfect life. It means teaching them how to lead a good and happy life in our imperfect world...Unknown. Don't take life to seriously, it isn't permanent!...By Sue Fitzmaurice. Find a peaceful place daily and let yourself grow...By Sue Fitzmaurice.

"The cost of ambition is late nights, and early mornings, loads of associates and very few friends. You will be misunderstood and you will be single unless, you are lucky enough to find someone who understands your lifestyle, other people in your field will want you to do good but never better than them, and for those reasons, you will do many things alone"...By soambitious@pharrell.

"It takes, nothing to join the crowd, it takes everything to stand alone"... By Hans. F. Hansen. "I don't engage in acts of kindness to be rewarded later, I engage in acts of kindness because it makes me feel good to give...Unknown. And always listen carefully to how a person speaks about other people to you because this is how they will speak about you to others but also make sure you don't comment on what they say about the person they are talking about to you, rather tell them you are not interested in discussing people...By Vincent Happy Mnisi.

"Your mind is not a cage, it is a garden, and it requires cultivating"...By Libba Bray. If you don't go after what you want, you will never get it, if you don't ask you will never know the answer and if don't stand up for what you believe in you are a coward...By Vincent Happy Mnisi. Somebody is out there somewhere thinking of you and the impact you made in their life...it's not me...l.o.l...but I think you are an idiot for not realizing it...By Vincent Happy Mnisi.

Hold onto your vision, every single one of us is blessed with powerful vision from God, but many of us have trouble holding on to them, so if you're a writer and you dream the plot to a novel write it down the second you wake up, maybe you're a singer and an amazing melody comes into your head while you're in your car tape it on your phone, don't assume you will remember it later. A lot of our best ideas can get lost in the distractions of the world, so if you have an idea even if you have to write it down in your kids crayons make sure you capture it, freeze it in your mind and meditate on it every day, because that vision is what is going to carry you to success...By Russell Simmons.

Making a big change is scary, but know what's even scarier? Regret...By Postivelifetips.com. The best days of your life begin today! Know that your kindness has a ripple effect in the universe...By Billy Cox. Be kind to you, the way you treat yourself will determine how everyone else treats you. Be kind to you...By LyndaFieldlifeCoach. Perfection is shallow, unreal and totally uninteresting...By Anne Lamoff. Tests and trails are meant for your belief. A failure to act faith nullifies our prayer...By T.B Joshua.

To get over the past, you first have to accept that the past is over. No matter how many times you revisit it, analyse it, regret it or sweat it...it's over. It can't hurt you no more...By Mandy Hale. Boundaries are part of self-care. They are healthy, normal and necessary...By Doreen Virtue. I can because I believe I can...By Lynda Fields Life-coach. You know everything is easier said than done. Don't give yourself that excuse!...By Sue Fitzmaurice.

Pause and remember if you just keep moving forward, everything you need will show up for you at the perfect time...By Senni Young. We can learn from a teacher, but in-order to master we must become the teacher. Never let your past dictate your future...By Billy Cox. You don't have a soul, you are a soul. You have a body...By Walter M. Miller.

When the voice of doubt start whispering, turn up the volume of faith and listen to your heart...By Bryant McGill. Where you start is not nearly as important as where you finish...By Zig Ziglar. Your hardest times often lead to the greatest moments of your life. Keep the faith, it will be worth it in the end...By Zig Ziglar. Ask yourself what is really important, and then have the wisdom and courage to build your life around your answer...By Energy Therapy. Always pray to have eyes that see the best, a heart that forgives the worst, a mind that forgets the bad and a soul that never loses faith...By rawforbeauty.com. Not everything that is faced can be changed. But nothing can be changed until it is faced...By James Baldwin.

A system cannot fail those it was never meant to protect...By W.E.B Dubious. Today is the oldest you've ever been and the youngest you will ever be, live life to the fullest today with no regrets...By Teamgrowingbolder.com And there is still a lot to learn and there is always great stuff out there, even mistakes can be wonderful...By Sifiso. E. Ntuli. Too often we underestimate the power of a touch, a smile, a kind word, a listening ear, an honest compliment, or the smallest act of caring, all of which the potential to turn a life around...By Leo Buscaglia. Don't be taken hostage by your negative thoughts, you can change your mood by changing your thoughts...By Lynda Fields. Sometimes it's not about finding answers; sometimes it's about facing them...By Sue Fitzmaurice.

Just because we're in a stressful situation doesn't mean that we have to get stressed out. You may be in the storm, the key is don't let the storm get in you...By Joel Osteen. If you can't explain it to a six year old, chances are you don't understand it yourself...By Ms Gloriah D.E. Life is a gift, and it offers us the privilege, opportunity and responsibility to give something back by becoming more...By Anthony Robbins.

If we do not feel grateful for what we already have, what makes us think we'd be happy with more...By Oprah Winfrey. Do something personally good for you, no one has to know. Like cleaning out a closet, you feel better after removing the clutter, even though no one else notices...By Anna Pereira. We are alive and we need to take risks. And if we fail, so what? Who cares? It doesn't matter. We learn and we move on without judgement...By Don Miguel Ruiz. There is a big difference between hearing your inner voice and listening to it...By Sonia Choquette.

I am not in a competition with anyone else. I run my own race. I have no desire to play the game of being better than everyone else around me in any way, shape of form. I just aim to improve, to become a better person than I was. That's me and I'm free...By Herty Borngreat Music. Getting knocked down in life is a given...getting up and moving forward is a choice...By Zig Ziglar. Do not delay the difficult decision or avoid the new habits that are necessary to advance your life. What must be done should be done with haste, for life is precious ...By Brendon Burchard. I 'm on a journey I've not taken before. I'm figuring it out as I go...By Sue Fitzmaurice. Of all the attitudes we can acquire, surely the attitude of gratitude is the most important and by far the most life changing ...By Zig Ziglar. "I don't regret the things I've done, I regret the things I didn't do when I had the chance...By Rich Mind Rich Man...

Believe there is a great power silently working all things for good, behave yourself and never mind the rest...By Beatrix Potter. If you tell the truth you don't have to remember anything...By Mark Twain. When life is joyous, the light will be there. When there is hardship the light will also be there...By Billy Fingers. Happiness keeps you sweet. Trials keep you strong. Sorrow keeps you human. Failure keeps you humble. And courage keeps you going...Unknown.

Over-thinking is the biggest cause of out unhappiness. Keep yourself occupied. Keep your mind off things that don't help you, stay focused and think positive…By Killian F. Bukutu. You can never make the same mistake twice because the second time you make it, it's not a mistake, it's a choice…By Baisden Live. The greatest pleasure in life is doing what people say you cannot do…By Baisden Live. And achieving what people said you can't achieve…By Vincent Happy Mnisi. Admit it? Admit it you aren't the same person you were a year ago…By Baisden Live. Take time every day to do what makes your soul smile…By Power of Positivity. Stop being afraid of what could go wrong and start being positive about what could go right…By Positive Life.

If in our daily life we can smile, if we can be peaceful and happy not only we, but everyone will profit from it. This is the most basic kind of peace work"…By Tich Nhat Hanh. The number one skill in life is not giving up…By Bryant McGill. I didn't give up, I just let go of the things that brought me down…By Perseverance Wakwa Mdluli. If you only knew the real power of your thoughts you would be very careful not to engage in negativity. Train your mind and turn to the positive at all times…By Lyndafiels.com. It's time to forgive yourself for that one thing you keep beating yourself up for…By www.projectforgive.com. Being happy doesn't mean that everything is perfect, it simply means that you've decided to look beyond the imperfections in life…By WomenWorking.com

I didn't have time but I made time. I didn't have the knowledge, but I did what I knew. I didn't have the support, but I learned to support myself. I didn't have the confidence but the confidence came with results. I had a lot going against me but I had enough going for me. I had plenty of excuses but I chose not to use any of them…By Billy Cox Motivation.

The strongest factor for success is self-esteem; believing you can do it, believing you deserve it, believing you will get it…By Billy Cox Motivation. Rejecting negative temptation is a sign of courage. Doing what is right and good is a sign of wisdom…By Mike Matongo. Be you! Do what you were called to. Be who you were called to be. You came in alone, and you will leave alone. Make sure you live your best life between those dates…By Tony Gaskins.

"The most important thing is to enjoy your life...to be happy...it's all that matters ...By Audrey Hepburn. Because the more you complain about your problems, the more problems you will have to complain about ...by Zig Ziglar. If you are reading this...Congratulations, you're alive. If that's not something to smile about then I don't know what is...By Baisden Live. For anyone who is waiting for when the time is right to go for their dreams. The news is: NOW!!! Is the time, Just Do It NOW!!!...By Lynda Fields. Let us live the day to the fullest, and never miss a chance to let those dearest to us know of our love for them...By Killian F. Bukutu. Dare to believe something amazing is going to happen in your life. When you believe all things are possible...By Joel Osteen. Our state of mind determines our state of being...By Spirit Science.

Things are going to get better hold your head up...By Earnest Pugh.com. Just be yourself, focused, confident, relaxed, kind, happy, motivated, brilliant, calm, free, inspired, creative, in control, amazing, appreciative, fabulous and energetic...By Vincent Happy Mnisi. Life is about balance...Be kind, don't let people abuse you. Trust, but don't be deceived. Be content, but never stop improving yourself...By PositiveLifeTips.com. If you are tired of starting over, stop giving up...By Dophin. Follow the **F.A.C.T.S** to be happy: **F**orget the past; **A**ccept your mistakes; **C**ry and move on; **T**hank God always; **S**mile Always...By SimpleBhangra,com.

Good parenting does not mean giving them a perfect life. It means teaching them how to lead a good and happy life in our imperfect world...Unknown. Don't take life to seriously, it isn't permanent!...By Sue Fitzmaurice. Find a peaceful place daily and let yourself grow...By Sue Fitzmaurice. Sometimes the most important thing in a whole day is the rest we take between two deep breaths...By Etty Hillesum.

Sometimes the hardest person to forgive is yourself. Once you do though, you set your soul free! So let go of the pain, shame and blame and truly live your life!...By Katy Gill-Marcusseno. Bad habits are like a comfortable bed, easy to get into, but hard to get out of...By I love being Black.com. Every positive thought is a silent prayer which will change your life...By Bryant McGill.

I relax and enjoy life. I know that whatever I need to know is revealed to me in the perfect time and space sequence...By Louise Hay. Some people don't want to see you blessed and living your life on new levels. They enjoy seeing you struggle. Now let them see your success, live your life!...By Tony Gaskins. And learn to learn something new each day, What does reading and writing teach us?? First and foremost, it reminds us that we are alive and that it is a gift and a privilege not a right...By Vincent Happy Mnisi.

May your life preach, more loudly than your lips...By Project-Forgive. If we look at our lives we will see that most of the time we do things just to please others, just to be accepted by others, rather than living our lives to please ourselves...By Don Miguel Ruiz. A positive thinker rises above self doubt and has the strength and character to overcome life's challenges. Are you a positive thinker?...By Lynda Fields. Life is to short to be serious all the time...So if you can't laugh at yourself, call me. I'll laugh at you...By Fifi and Dave. Your life is going in the direction of your dominant thought...By Andrew Wommack. Living the dream isn't always about amassing wealth or going on fancy trips...it's about sharing what's alive in your heart with the world....By Molly Hahn.

We all have times when life feels hard; when we're frustrated and tired and just want to hide away. If that's you right now, don't worry every caterpillar has to rest to become a butterfly and you'll soon find your wings again. In the mean time, let your Angels wrap you in theirs. You are loved...By Anna Taylor. The five **W**'s of life; **W**ho you are is what makes you special. Do not change for anyone. **W**hat lies ahead will always be a mystery. Do not be afraid to explore...**W**hen life pushes you over, push back harder. **W**here there are choices to make, make the one you won't regret. **W**hy things happen will never be certain take it in stride and move forward...Unknown

Sure sign of spiritual growth; is when you realise how challenging it is to change yourself and you begin to understand what little chance you have in trying to change others...By renewed Mind. Life is really very simple. What we give out, we get back. Every thought we think is creating our future...By Louise Hay.

Success is not the key to happiness. Happiness is the key to success, if you love what you are doing, you'll be a success...By Brain Tracy. I am not here to be average, I am here to be awesome...By Power of positivity.com.

Every struggle in your life has shaped you into the person you are today. Be thankful for the hard times, they can only make you stronger...Unknown. Grant me the strength to focus this week, to be mindful and present, to serve with excellence, to be a force of love...By Brendon Burchard. I'd rather have a life of "Oh Wells" than a life of "What ifs...Baisden Live.

Educating the mind without educating the heart is no education at all...By Aristotle. Purpose, it's just a word, so is living, loving, laughing, forgiving...All will work out! Don't be so intimidated by one small word...By Anna Pereira. Life is so ironic...It takes sadness to know what happiness is, noise to appreciate silence and absence to value presence...Unknown. Three simple rules of life; If you don't go after what you want, You'll never have it; If you don't ask, the answer will always be No; If you don't step forward, you will always be in the same place...By Vincent Happy Mnisi. Everyday is chance to change your life. Take this chance today...By Lynda Fields

Don't "GO" through life, "Grow" through life. Realise the journey of life is not about being right or pretending to know it all. It's about learning and growing every step of the way...By Dan Zadra. Life is about learning and growing...By Vincent Happy Mnisi. Just because we're in a stressful situation doesn't mean that we have to get stressed out. You may be in the storm. The key is, don't let the storm get in you...By Joel Osteen.  If you want to fly, give up everything that weighs you down...By Music for Deep Meditations.

One day you will wake up and realise that life has passed you by, that your dreams of today are gone, that the things you wanted are no longer there. Not today. Not now. Not your life. This is the day where you take control and create your future. Life isn't about waiting, hoping or wishing. It is about creating, doing and truly living. Today is that Day...By Brad Gast.

If wishes were horse beggars would ride, you have to work at what you want out of life which in-turn creates you future...By Vincent Happy Mnisi. Instead of wishing your life was different, wish for courage, strength, motivation and a great sense of humour. With all those things you can change it yourself...By Mindful Wishes.

A positive thinker rises above self-doubt and has the strength of character to overcome life's challenges. Are you a Positive thinker?...By Lynda Fields. Reach deep down in yourself and discover that person that can make a difference in life...By Vincent Happy Mnisi. There is a truth deep down inside of you that has been waiting for you to discover it, and that truth is this: You deserve all good things life has to offer...By Rhonda Byrne. Cultivate the habit of being grateful for every good thing that comes to you, and to give thanks continuously. And because all things have contributed to your advancement, you should include all things in your gratitude...By Rolph Waldo Emerson.

10 ways to stay Optimistic 1)Decide to be Happy. 2)Expect the best. 3)Trust the Universe 4)Look for the Silver Lining. 5)Celebrate life. 6)Take a Positive view. 7)Don't forget to have some fun! 8)Make each day count. 9)Be an Encourager 10)Appreciate yourself...By Lynda Fields. The secret to Happiness: Be good to yourself, be true to yourself and love who you are right now...By Lisa Prosen.

Gratitude unlocks the fullness of life. It turns what we have into enough, and more. It turns denial into acceptance, chaos to order, confusion to clarity. Gratitude makes sense of our past, brings peace to today and creates a vision for tomorrow...By Melody Beattle. Success is not determined by the outcome. The outcome is the result of having decided that you are successful to begin with...By T.F Hodge. The quality of our actions depends on our motivation. A real appreciation of humanity, compassion and love are crucial to this. Whether we work in science; agriculture; or politics, if we're good hearted about it our contribution will be positive...By The Dalai Lama.

Sometimes it's important to work for that pot of Gold. But other times it's essential to take time off and to make sure that your most important decision in the day simply consists of choosing which colour to slide down on the Rainbow...By Douglas Pagels.

At the end of life, what really matters is not what we bought, but what we built. Not what we got, but what we shared. Not our competence, but our character, and not our success, but our significance. Live a life that matters. Live a life of love...Unknown. "Now and then it's good to pause in our pursuit of happiness and just be happy"...By Guillaume Apollinaire.

Life isn't about getting and having, it's about giving and being...By Kevin Kruse. Happiness is finding yourself...By Happy Page. As long as you are above ground and breathing, there is a beautiful purpose for you on this earth. Never give up on your life!...By Maria, Mystic Sounds. Life is hard but so very beautiful...By Abraham Lincoln. The key to happiness is to allow yourself to be immersed in the joys of life. Let your light shine through your attitude be yourself, beautiful; Believe in yourself, have the courage to create and dream. Be honest, kind and always hope for happiness. Put passion into everything you do, with strength and sear persistence and you, will surely succeed. Have faith in your destiny and always give as it's good for the soul...By Soul Sensation.

Life is short...Laugh, be grateful! Breathe Deep, Appreciate, Hug Tight, Keep Promise, Dream Big, Share Happiness, Love Unconditionally, Make Wishes, Help Others, Do Your Best, Have Hope, Keep Your Chin Up, Speak Kindly, Play, Cherish, Read, Smile...Unknown. You are the Champion of your life. Every champion has been knocked down, bruised, bumped, underestimated, and many times, felt like giving up. A Champion is not measured by strength, intelligence, luck or acclaim. A Champion is made up of heart, will and determination to continue, no matter what. Always remember you can and you will make it...By Doe Zantamata. Life is short. If there was ever a moment to follow your passion and do something that matters to you, that moment is now...By Baisden Live.

You must give up the life you planned. In-order to have the life that is waiting for you...By Joseph Campbell. Let your faith be bigger than your fear...By Music for Deep Meditation. Pause and Remember-The peace you seek begins with you! When you consciously and consistently choose peace in your words and actions, more peace will appear in your life. Stop blaming everything and everyone outside of you. Make peace within your priorities...By Senni Young.

Spreading kindness sets my heart of fire...in a totally good way...By Hoods Kindness Revolution Experiment. Joyful wishes for a day, a week, a month, a year...By Life overflowing with happy surprises! I choose to make the rest of my life the best of my life...By Louise Hay. When you do what you love, and love what you do, you'll have success, Your whole life through...Greg S. Reid.

A good life is when you assume nothing, do more, need less, smile often, dream big, laugh a lot and realize how blessed you are to be living your life...By Vincent Happy Mnisi. Sometimes all you need is a hundred million dollars...By Sue Fitzmaurice. My mission in life is not merely to survive, but the thrive; and to do so with some passion, some compassion, some humour, and some style...By Maya Angelou. The number one skills in life is not giving up...Bryant McGill. Seven things that you have to give up to get your life on track 1) Stop pleasing people for the sake of pleasing them. 2) Doubting yourself. 3) Negative thinking 4) Fear of failure 5) Criticizing yourself and others. 6) Saying yes when you wanted to say no. 7)Procrastination yes we all suffer from it. You've been criticizing yourself for years and it hasn't worked, try approving of yourself and see what happens By Louise Hay.

My mission in life is not merely to survive, but to thrive; and do so with some passion, some compassion. Some humour and some style...By Maya Angelou. Success and fulfilment in life rests on the unflagging ability to get up, to be ourselves, to chase our dreams with fire each day, to keep willing ourselves to the next level of presence and performance and potential...By Brendon Burchard. You are a living magnet. What you attract into your life is in harmony with your dominant thoughts...By Basiden Live.

The great joys in life come when we are spontaneous and authentic while engaging in activities we care about. And the great miseries come when to many days stack up when we are conforming and posing while doing things we have no passion for....By Brendon Burchard. Strength does not come from wining. Your struggles develop your strengths. When you go through hardships and decide no to surrender, that is strength...By Mohandas Gandhi.

Avoiding danger is no safer in the long run than outright exposure, life is either a daring adventure or nothing...By Helen Keller. We all have been placed on this earth to discover our own path and we'll never be happy if we live someone else's idea of life....By The PowerWithin. Not everyone will understand your journey, it's not theirs to make sense of. It is your life...By Vincent Happy Mnisi.

It's pretty awesome the way things work out a lot of the time but not always. Sometimes things suck and the only positive spin we can give them is that we're sure to grow from the pain of it all that nothing is for nothing and in its own way that's pretty awesome too...By Scott Stabile.

By Changing your mindset and attitude, you might just change your life, You don't have to have it all figured out to move forward,just have faith in God and believe in yourself. Keep Moving...Champion Mode...By Rato KasiSoul Molaba. Acknowledging the good that you already have in your life is the foundation for all abundance...By Eckhart Tolle.

To make the right choices in life, you have to get in touch with your soul. To do this you need to experience solitude, which most people are afraid of because in the silence you hear the truth and know the solutions...By Deepak Chopra. Quit worrying about how everything is going to turn out. Live one day at a time, better yet, make the most of this moment...By Joel Osteen.

Whatever life may send your way...Make the Best of it. Don't waste your time and energy worrying about it, instead find a way to do something about it. Learn from it, adjust to it, be strong, be flexible and be your best in very situation. Wisdom is nothing more than healed pain...By Charles Glassman.

You were put on this earth to achieve your greatest self, to live out your purpose and to do it fearlessly...By Steve Maroboli. The real secret to a fabulous life is to live imperfectly with Great delight...By Leigh Standley.

I can't quit now. I can't let it break my spirit. I can't let hate control me, I have to keep fighting the good fight and know that one day my voice will count and my life will matter!...By Tony Gaskins. You know when the path you are walking is healing you, because you stop looking back at what happened and start looking forward to what's coming...By Kate Spencer.

There are Four very Important words in life, LOVE; HONESTY; TRUTH; and RESPECT!. Without these in your life, you have nothing...By Pinoy Rap Radio. Laugh when you can, apologise when you should and let go of what you can't change. Kiss slowly, play hard, forgive quickly, take chances, give everything and have no regrets. Life's too short to be anything...but Happy...Unknown.

Here's the truth your situation is never permanent it's what you make it. Life isn't solid, it's fluid. It changes. Life is not about the answer. The lesson, the curiosities. The opening up to awareness, its what evolves us one by one. This is how we live life...By Anna Pereira.

Don't wait for everything to be prefect before you decide to enjoy your life...By Joyce Meyer. Acknowledging the good that you already have in your life is the foundation for all abundance...By Eckhart Tolle. Your life is always a perfect reflection of your state of mind and of your truest identity...By Bryant McGill.Happiness isn't about getting what you want all the time. It's about loving what you have and being grateful for it...Unknown. At some point you just have to let go what you thought should happen and live in what is happening...By Codeblack Life.

I want to change the world. But I have found that the only thing one can be sure of changing is oneself...By Aldus Huxley. Life is short, live it. Love is rare, cherish it. Dreams are real, follow them. Memories are magic, make them. People matter, show them. Kindness counts, be it...By Happygohappygolucky.

Your life begins to change the day you take responsibility for it...By Steve Maroboli. Your greatest self has been waiting your whole life; don't make it wait any longer...By Steve Maroboli. Life without problems is a school without lessons...By Livelifehappy.com.

As I make more and more positive changes, my life just gets better and better...By Lynda Fields. Life's greatest difficulties always happen right before life's greatest breakthroughs...By Billy Cox. Remember without difficulties times in your life, you wouldn't be who you are today. Be grateful for the good and the bad...By Steven Aitchison. When you focus on problems, you'll have more problems when you focus on possibilities you'll have more opportunities...By Kushandwizdom.

The best things are free, And it is important never to lose sight of that. So look around you. Wherever you see friendship, loyalty, laughter and love...there is your treasure...By Heale Donald Walsch. Life is an echo. What you send out comes back. What you sow, you reap. What you give, you get. What you see in others exists in you...By Zig Ziglar.

When you feel self-doubt, fear and negativity arising just take a moment to stop and to remind yourself that these feelings are only the result of your thoughts, remember that you can change your thoughts and this way you can change the quality of your life...By Lynda Fields. Being happy doesn't mean that everything is perfect, it simply means that you've decided to look beyond imperfections in life...By WomenWorking.com.

# Chapter 3: The Company you keep!?...

"FRIENDS ARE THE FAMILY WE CHOOSE FOR OURSELVES THEY ARE LIKE THE SUNSHINE THAT BRIGHTENS UP OUR DAY...AND I BET YOU AGAIN THAT IF YOU PRAY TO GOD TO PROTECT YOU FROM YOUR ENEMIES, THAT YOU WILL START LOSING PEOPLE YOU THOUGHT WERE YOUR FRIENDS." YESTERDAY I WAS CLEVER, SO I WANTED TO CHANGE THE WORLD...TODAY I AM WISER, SO I AM CHANGING MYSELF. A PERFECT PERSON DOESN'T SMOKE, DOESN'T DRINK, DOESN'T CRY, DOESN'T FAIL AND DOESN'T EXIT...BY VINCENT HAPPY MNISI. LIFE'S TOO SHORT TO ARGUE AND FIGHT. COUNT YOUR BLESSINGS VALUE YOUR FRIENDS AND MOVE ON WITH YOUR HEAD HELD HIGH AND SMILE FOR EVERYONE...BY ONE SPARK FOUNDATION.

"You cannot hang out with negative people and expect to live a positive life" By Joel Osteen. "Avoid negative people, for they are the greatest destroyers of self-confidence and self-esteem, surround yourself with people who bring out the best in you"...by Billy Cox. Family isn't always blood, it's the people in your life who want you in theirs; the ones who accept you for who you are, the ones who would do anything to see you smile and who love you no matter what...by Vincent Happy Mnisi. You see a person's true colours when you are no longer beneficial to their life...By Vincent Happy Mnisi. "I don't care about losing people who don't wanna be in my life anymore. I've lost people who meant the world to me and I am still doing fine"...By Vincent Happy Mnisi. "I don't know the key to success, but the key to failure is to try and please everyone". By Bill Cosby.

Become friends with people who aren't your age. Hang out with people whose first language isn't the same as yours. Get to know someone who doesn't come from your social class. This is how you see the world. This is how you grow...By Sanaa Lathan. Speak when you are angry and you will make the best speech you will never regret...By Abrose Bierce.

Tact is the ability to tell someone to go to hell in such a way that they look forward to the trip...By Vincent Happy Mnisi. "People were created to be loved; things were created to be used. The reason why this world is in chaos is because things are being loved and people are being used"...By The Mind Unleashed. "I fall, I rise, I make mistakes, I live, I learn, I am not perfect but I am thankful"...By Trina

"Sometimes our lives have to be completely shaken up, changed, and rearranged to relocate us to the place we are meant to be". By Quote's' Thoughts. Those who sow in tears shall reap in joy...Psalm 126:5.A person, who has good thoughts, cannot ever be ugly. You can have a wonky nose and a crooked mouth and a double chin and stick-out teeth, but if you have good thoughts they will shine out of your face like sunbeams and you will always look lovely...Unknown. Surround yourself with only people who are going to lift you higher...By Oprah Winfrey.

"When the blood in your veins returns to the sea, and the earth in your bones returns to the ground, perhaps then you will remember that this land does not belong to you, it is you who belongs to this land"..Indian proverb. Be the reason someone smiles today...Unknown. It's been said that everlasting friends go long periods of time without speaking and never question their friendship. These friends pick up phones like they just spoke yesterday, regardless of how long it has been or how far away they live and they don't hold grudges. They understand that life is busy and you will always love them...By Vincent Happy Mnisi

"The world's going to judge you no matter what you do, so live life the way you fucking want too". By Rihanna. I don't live my life to please anyone, I don't care what anyone thinks. If you don't like me don't talk to me problem solved"...Right!?Right!...By Vincent Happy Mnisi. "I think it's very healthy to spend time alone. You need to know how to be alone and not be defined by another person"...By Oscar Wilde. "If you think adventure is dangerous, try routine, it is lethal". By Paulo Coelho.

"Happiness starts with you, not with your relationship, not with your job, not with your money, but with you. By Basiden Live. "Be thankful for what you have; you will end up having more. If you concentrate on what you don't have, you will never ever have enough"...By Oprah Winfrey. Two things define you. Your patience when you have nothing, and your attitude when you have everything...By Where the is love there is life. "Happiness is not something that you get in life...Happiness is rather something that you bring to life...By Vincent Happy Mnisi. Sometimes you have to forget what you want, to remember what you deserve"...By Killian F. Bhukutu.

"The less people you chill with, the less bullshit you deal with...By 9Gags. "Sometimes you have to move on without certain people, If they are meant to be in your life, they will catch up"...by Mandy Hale. "It's during the worst times of your life that you will get to see the true colours of the people who say they care for you" by Bobby Valintino. "Everything happens for a reason, maybe you don't see the reason right now, but when it is finally revealed...it will blow you away...By Baisden Live.

Sometimes you just, have to close your eyes, count to ten, take a deep breath, remind yourself that you wouldn't look good in a prison uniform and just smile at that dumb-ass and walk away...Unknown. "The truth does not change because it is, or is not believed by the majority of the people...By Giordan Bruno "The truth will always remain the truth and it will set you free" By Vincent Happy Mnisi. "When your past calls don't answer. It has nothing new to say...By Basiden Live.

"The most dangerous liars are those who think they are telling the truth". By Baisden Live. The worst person to be around is someone who complains about everything and appreciates nothing...By Baisden Live. "We are all going to die, all of us, what a circus! That alone should make us love each other but it doesn't. We are terrorized and flattened by trivialities, we are eaten up by nothing...By Charles Bukowski.

Returning hate for hate multiplies hate, adding deeper darkness to a night already devoid of stars...By Martin Luther King Jr. You have to speak to be heard, but sometimes you have to be silent to be appreciated. The most hurtful thing you can say to someone is to say nothing...Unknown. "If you want to live a happy life tie it to a goal, not to people and things"...By Albert Einstein

Sometimes I forget to thank the people who make my life happy in some many ways. Sometimes I forget to tell them how much I really do appreciate them for being an important part of my life. So thank you all of you, just for being here for me...by Healing Hugs. I like those friends that you don't have to talk to everyday but you're still friends even if you go weeks without talking to each other...By Trent Shelton. Sometimes the more chances you give the more respect you lose. Never let a person get comfortable with disrespecting you...By #RehabTime.

"What kept me sane was knowing that things would change, and it was a question of keeping myself together until they did...By Nina Simone. "Some people come in your life as blessings, others come in your life as lessons. By Baisden Live. "Life is short, there is no time to leave important words unsaid"...By Vincent Happy Mnisi. "But before an individual can be saved, he must first learn that he cannot save himself"...By M.R Dehaan M.D

"Everybody has a good story to tell about their life"...By Vincent Happy Mnisi. "People think being alone makes you lonely, but I don't think that's true, being surrounded by the wrong people is the loneliest thing in the world"...By Kim Culbertson. "Life is better when you're laughing". By Vincent Happy Mnisi. "Good things come to those who believe, better things come to those who are patient and the best things come to those who don't give up"...By Vincent Happy Mnisi "May your life preach more loudly than your lips...By William Ellery Channing.

Take care of your thoughts when you are alone, and take care of your words when you are with people"...By Vincent Happy Mnisi. "Our culture has accepted two huge lies, first is that if you disagree with someone's lifestyle, you must fear or hate them. The second is that to love someone means you must agree with everything they believe in or do. Both are nonsense. You don't have to compromise convictions to be compassionate" By Rick Warren. We are pressured, but not crushed; perplexed, but not frustrated, persecuted but not abandoned..2 Corinthians 4:8-9.

"The approval fix, do the best you can, be the best that you can be and do not feel you should be able to do more just because someone else does more. Just be yourself, and don't pressure yourself to perform exactly the way others do...By Joyce Meyers.

There are people who have plotted against you who still don't know how you survived...By Lil O. Real situations expose fake people, rock bottom will always reveal what's real...By Trent Shelton. Your hardest times will expose your truest friendships, Rock bottom will always reveal who's real. Know your circle...By RehabTime. Sometimes you just need to disconnect and enjoy your own company...By Daily Dose.

Let wisdom be your sister and knowledge your friend...Proverbs 7 v 4. Wanted: Encourages (We have a surplus of critics already, thanks...By The World. "All views are entitled to be aired. It is through vigorous and constructive debate that together we will chart the path ahead"...By Nelson Rolihlahla Mandela. Whoever controls the media, controls the culture"...by Allen Ginsberg. "When your earnings are exhausted on food and shelter, your labours are no longer viewed as an opportunity for economic advancement, but rather as an act of self-preservation. In the real world, that's called slavery...By Vincent Happy Mnisi. "I found the key to happiness stay away from idiots"...By Susan Anderson.

"Finish every day, and be done with it...You have done what you could...some blunders and absurdities no doubt crept in, forget them as fast as you can, tomorrow is a new day. You shall begin it well and serenely, and with to high a spirit to cumbered with your old nonsense"...By Ralph Waldo Emerson.

10 ways to move on 1) Allow yourself to be happy. 2) Be confident and trust yourself. 3) Welcome change and go with it. 4) Be courage's and take a risk. 5) Ditch the guilt. 6) Know that you deserve the best. 7)Make a decision and follow it through. 8) Smile in the face of adversity. 9) Remember that you are good enough. 10) Be yourself...Unknown .

"Sometimes deciding to quit something is the most remarkably bold and courage's thing you can do. If it's not right for you, if it is sapping your spirit and not part of your ideal vision for your future, then it is something to quit and quit soon"...By Brendon Burchard. "People come and go from our lives all the time, it not our fault that people leave. The universe is just making room for new people with new lessons"...By Sue Fitzmaurice.

"Life becomes easier when you learn to accept the apology you never got"...By Robert Brault. And "If you are doing the best you can under your current circumstances...then kick up your heels and dance... By Zen to Zany. True friends don't believe rumours about you because they know you. True friends defend you, and not help spread lies about you...By Rehabitime...

Sometimes the bad things that happen in our life's put us directly on the path to the best things that will ever happen to us...By Bruce Tiberg. "When the world says "Give up" Hope whispers "One more time"...Unknown.

The secret to change is to focus all your energy, not on fighting the old, but on building the new"...By Socrates. If you want to live your dreams, you have to give up all your excuses. By Brad Sugars. Ego says "Once everything falls into place, I will find peace" Spirit says "Find peace and everything will fall into place". If you want to reach a goal you must see the reaching of that goal in your mind before you actually arrive at your goal...By Zig Ziglar. "Once you feel you are avoided by someone, never disturb them again...By Wyn and Wilson. Get your hustle on...Hard work is easy, working out is hard...There are something's that money cannot buy, like manners, morals, intelligence and class...By Virgin Radio Lebanon. "Try being informed instead of just opinionated. And tell the negative committee that meets inside your head to sit down and shut up...By Ann Bradford.

Success means doing the best we can with what we have. Success is the doing, not the getting; in the trying, not the triumph. Success is personal standard reaching for the highest that is in us, becoming all that we can be...By Zig Ziglar.

God often uses our deepest pain as the launching pad of our greatest calling..."Mistakes have the power to turn you into something better than you were before...Unknown. Life is give and take, don't lose the battle in your mind. Always remember; the more life stresses you, the more life will have to bless you. Get ready to receive your blessings...By Tony Gaskins. "In the end, we only regret the chances we didn't take, relationships we were afraid to have, and the decisions we waited too long to make"...By John Tesh. "Choose to win each day, defy the odds, embrace challenges, and never let adversity steal your dreams"...By Billy Cox.

A change begins in your mind...by Billy Cox. If you are grateful for even one thing in your life right now, there is no need to regret the past because it brought you here, embrace your journey...by Anna Taylor.

You can't play it safe your whole life and expect to reach your highest potential. You've got to be willing to take some risk...By Joel Osteen ministries. Weak people revenge, strong people forgive, intelligent people ignore...By Earnest Pugh.

"When people don't know what's going on in your life, they speculate...when they think they know...they fabricate and when they do know...they just hate"...By Baisden Live. "Never give up on what you really want to do, the person with big dreams is more powerful than one with facts...by Albert Einstein. Having a friend who understands your tears is much more valuable than having a bunch of friends who only know your smile...By #RehabTime.

I am strong, I am resilient, I try my best, I value my life, I am not perfect, I am the perfect me, I never give up, I am empathetic, I am a warrior ready to conquer. I am not broken, I am together. I take things one day at a time, I'm independent, and I'm human. I'm a survivor." "A man who isolates himself seeks his own desires, he rages against all wise judgement...A fool has no delight in understanding, but in expressing his own heart...From Bible Proverbs 18 V 1&2.

"The person you took for granted today, may turn out to be the person you need tomorrow, be careful how you treat people"...By Biasden Live. Spiritually, it's important to forgive those who hurt you, but you don't need to hang out with them...By Assertiveness for Earth Angles. The biggest communication problem is we do not listen to understand, instead we listen to reply. "You may control all the events, that happen to you, but you can decide not to be reduced by them...By Maya Angelou. We are very good lawyers for our own mistakes, but very good Judges for the mistakes of others...By Basiden Live. The strongest factor for success is self-esteem, believing you can do it, believing you deserve it, believing you will get it...By Vincent Happy Mnisi.

Never trust anyone who always blames everyone else for everything wrong in their life...By Anna Pereira. Not everything that is faced can be changed, but nothing can be changed until it is faced...By James Baldwin.

I was raised! I didn't just grow up, I was taught to speak when I enter a room. Say please and thank you, to have respect for my elders and to get up off my lazy butt and let the elders in the room have my chair, Say "Yes sir" and "No sir", lend a helping hand to those in need. Hold the door for the person behind me, say excuse me when it's needed, and to love people for who they are and not for what I can get from them, I was also taught to treat people the way I wanted to be treated...By Right Wings News.

It does not matter if a million people tell you what you can't do, or if 10 million tell you "No". If you get one "Yes" from God, that's all you need...By Tyler Perry. When you do the right thing in the right way, you have nothing to lose because you have nothing to fear...By Zig Ziglar. You have never really lived until you have done something for someone who can never repay you...By Baisden Live.

Many people, especially ignorant people, want to punish you for speaking the truth, for being correct, or for being years ahead of your time. If you are right and you know it, speak your mind. Even if you are a minority of one, the truth is still the truth...by Gandhi. I regret nothing in my life even if my past was full of hurt, I still look back and smile, because it made me who I am today...By Vincent Happy Mnisi.

The way you dress yourself and portray yourself to the world says plenty about who you are and how you want the world to accept you...by Vincent Happy Mnisi. You never know what you can achieve until you have pushed yourself to your limit...By Vincent Happy Mnisi. "When writing the story of your life, don't let anyone else hold the pen. The best way to predict the future; it's to create one yourself"...By Sifiso Ntuli. "Success is no accident, it is hard work; perseverance; learning; studying; sacrifice and most of all love what you are doing or learning to do"...By Pele.

Don't look back and wonder why things went wrong, don't regret not doing more, it happened for a reason, your better days are ahead of you...By Killian Bukutu. Forget about all the reasons why something may not work, you only need to find one reason why it will...By Sifiso Ntuli.

I will no longer allow the negative things in my life to spoil all of the good things I have, I choose to be happy. I would rather be anointed by Jesus than be popular. The first to apologies is the bravest the first to forgive is strongest, and the first to forget is the happiest. Stop holding on to the wrong people. Let them go on their way; if not for you, then for them...By Bryant McGill.

Accept the person and the situation for exactly what it is instead of trying to manipulate it into what you think it needs to be...By Mandy Hale. Call me crazy but I love to see other people happy and succeeding...By Baisden Live.

Life is flying by, you don't have time to waste another minute being negative offended or bitter. If someone did you wrong, get over it and move forward...by Joel Osteen Ministries. I'm making some changes in my life. If you don't hear anything from me, you are one of them...By Baisden Live. I don't have to agree with you to like you or respect you...By Anthony Bourdain. I actually don't need to control my anger. Everyone around me needs to control their habits of pissing me off...By Baisden Live.

I have learned the value in experience, though I haven't always seen things clear, I'm now thankful for things I never imagined I could be. If it wasn't for the liars, I wouldn't know the value of peace. If it wasn't for the good things failing, I wouldn't know what was needed to set the foundations for something great. I learned the power of acceptance through my disappointments. Every

let-down has left me in a position to grow, and I'm wiser because of it all. I am proud of my heart, it's never been a quitter, it hasn't become bitter, it's had the courage to stay open, and that has only made me better...By Rob Hill Snr.

There is no passion to be found playing small in settling for a life that is less than the one you are capable of living...By Nelson Mandela. Do not judge me by my successes, judge me by how many times I fell down and got back up again...By Nelson Mandela.  There is no need to rush, if something is meant to be, it will happen in the right time, with the right person for the right reasons...By Vincent Happy Mnisi. Happiness does not depend on what you have or who you are; it solely relies on what you think...By Buddha. Everything you're going through is preparing you for what you asked for...By Kim Cole.

Wealth makes friends, but the poor is separated from his friends...Book of Proverbs The Bible. If you under attack, it's because your blessing is close; thieves only come to loaded vaults, stay encouraged...By Empowered woman of faith and purpose.

Stop holding on to the wrong people. Let them go on their own way; if not for you, then for them...By Bryant McGill. Always pray to have eyes that see the best, a heart that forgives the worst, a mind that forgets the bad and a soul that never loses faith...By rawforbeauty.com. Never trust anyone who blames everyone else for everything wrong in their life...By Anna Pereira.

Not everything that is faced can be changed, but nothing can be changed until it is faced...By James Baldwin. You will never understand a person until you consider things from their point of view, until you consider things from their point of view, until you climb into their skin and walk around in it...By Harper lee. Don't argue with fools, people passing by won't be able to tell who's who...By I love being black. You have permission to walk away from anything that doesn't feel right. Trust your instincts and listens to your inner voice. It's trying to protect you...By Bryant McGill.

Stop holding onto people who keep letting go of you. Pay attention to the faithful people. The ones you don't have to impress, the ones who always have your back. The ones that love you with no strings attached...By Tami Roman.

The best way to avoid disappointment, Is not to expect anything from anyone...By Simply Bhagra. Never cry for that person who doesn't know the value of your tears...By Baisden Live. Thanks for being my friend...By One Spark Foundation. I fall, I rise. I make mistakes. I live. I learn. I've been hurt but I'm alive. I'm human. I'm not perfect but I'm thankful...By Joy of Mom. It's double worrying to make someone happy, first you spend your efforts is the physical acts; then waste your mental energy stressing what if they still aren't happy; Cut your work in half by finding your worth through self-confidence. When you are happy with you, you will come together with those who will be happy to be with you. Stop people pleasing at the cost of your joy...By Anna Pererira.


I believe in second chances, I don't think everyone deserves them...By Baisden Live. Such a disappointment when you defend someone for so long think they are different and they turn out to be just like what everyone said...By Official KBLX fan page. You are not responsible for everyone else's happiness, only they can choose their mental state, you cannot choose for them!...By Lynda Fields Life Coach. If you can't appreciate you then let them miss you. Absence makes the heart grow fonder; But if theirs doesn't grow fonder, at least yours will grow stronger...By Tony Gaskins. I don't let people pull me into their storm; I pull them into my peace...By @Lourenleisbeg. The only people I owe my loyalty to those who never made me question theirs. One of the big lessons I have learned from my journey is you can't please everyone so don't try...By Bill Cosby. Surround yourself with people who clearly love your light and add to it...Unknown.

"Some people are allergic to nuts. Some people are allergic to milk, Me? I am allergic to bullshit and negativity"...By Tony. A Gaskin Jr. Successful people build each other up, they motivate, inspire and push each other. Unsuccessful people just hate, blame and complain...By Vicki Yohe. Fake people don't surprise me anymore, loyal people do...By Phuckyoquote. When you're dead, you don't know you're dead it's the same way when you're stupid...By Rottenecards. People often say that motivation doesn't last. Well neither does bathing...That's why we recommend it daily...By Zig Ziglar.

If you think everything is someone else's fault, you'd be wrong. But if you think that everything is your fault, you're also wrong. Assigning blame can keep you stuck in the problem. Move on to solutions...By Sue Fitzmaurice. Always help someone, you might the only one who does...Unknown.

Lord remove anybody out of my life that means me no good, serves me no good purpose, discernment to realise and give me the strength to let go and don't look back...By Dr Farah Gray. Other people and things can stop you temporarily. You're the only who can do it permanently...By Zig Ziglar. Nourish your soul by spending time with people that celebrate who you are, and avoid those that simply you tolerate. You are worth more than that…By Kate Spencer.

If you feel ignored, you're probably doing everything right…By Anna Pererira. Direction is so much more important than speed. Many are going nowhere fast…By The Mankind Project. Be careful who you trust. If someone will discuss others with you, they will certainly discuss you with others…By Baisden Live. Your circles of friends must match your own aspirations and dreams, or you will find little support when you need it most…By Leon Brown. You know my name, not my story. You've heard what I've done, not what I 've been through. If you were in my shoes you'd fall the first step…By Herty Borngreat Music. There comes a time when you have to stop crossing oceans for people who wouldn't jump puddles for you…By Dr Laura.

**F.R.I.E.N.D.S** **F**ight for you. **R**espect you. **I**nclude you. **E**ncourage you. **N**eed you. **D**eserve you. **S**tand by you…Unknown. Snakes don't hiss anymore with you to like you or respect you…By Anthony Bourdain.

Hear me when I tell you this: People who ignore you, until it suits them to talk to you, are not worth your friendship or your time!...By Baisden Live. Call me crazy but I love to see other people happy and succeeding…By Baisden Live. The best kind of people are the ones that come into your life, and make you see the sun where you once saw clouds. The people that believe in you so much, you start to believe in you too…The people that love you simply for being you. The once in a lifetime kind of people…By Baisden Live. Just be honest with me or stay away from me. It's not that difficult…By Baisden Live

People will question all the good things they hear about you but believe all the bad without a second thought…By Kevin Hart. Don't waste words on people who deserve your silence. Sometimes the most powerful thing you can say is nothing at all…By WisdomlifeQuotes.com.

You teach people how to treat you by what you allow, what you stop, and what you reinforce…By Tony Gaskins. I love straight people, makes life ten times easier…By Positive Life. If you set yourself free from what everyone else thinks and start being who you were created to be, you will rise to a new level…By Vincent Happy Mnisi….. When we are kind to ourselves and one another, we create heaven on earth…By…Earthlovers.com.

When you find yourself in the position to help someone, be happy and feel blessed because God is answering that person's pray, through you. Remember: Our purpose on earth is not to get lost in the dark but to be a light to others, so that they may find their way through us...God bless you...By Alberto Casing. "What is one thing you can do right now to makes someone's day better? Do it"...By Positive Thinking.

Everyone has experienced something that has changed them in a way that they could never go back to the person they once were...By Killian Bukutu. Always stay true to yourself and never let what somebody else says distract you from your goals...By Michelle Obama. In the end, people will judge you anyway. Don't live your life impressing others. Live your life impressing yourself...By rawforbeauty. Boys need face-to-face time with men because they need to see a good man to know how to become one...By Meg Meeker MD.com. The saddest thing about betrayal is that it never comes from your enemies...By Baisedn Live. There person you trusted may turn out to be your worst enemy...be careful of who you tell your secrets...By Vincent Happy Mnisi.

You can't use people and expect God to keep blessing you ...By Martin Lawrence. Some of the things we hold on to the most are the things we need to let go of the most...By Shawne Duperon. People, who are crazy enough to think they can change the world, are the ones who do...By Steve Jobs.

Successful people are always looking for opportunities to help others. Unsuccessful people are always asking "What's in it for me?"...By Brain Tracy. Every choice you make has an end result...By Zig Ziglar.

Remember that...Criticism, Negativity, spitefulness are only reflections of the person giving them. You don't have to accept them...By Zig Ziglar. If you want to fly, you have to give up the things that weigh you down...By Toni Morrison. Nobody is too busy; it's just a matter of priorities...By Brain Tracy.

Never be afraid to raise your voice for honesty and truth and compassion, against injustice and lying and greed. If people all over the world did this, it would change the Earth...By William Faulkner. Ego and greed work very well with each other, they are both never satisfied with what they have…By Nathan Sipho Banana KaNcube.

If you want to make peace with an enemy, one must work with that enemy and that enemy becomes your partner…By Nelson Mandela. When someone tells you, "You've changed" It might simply be because you've stopped living your life their way… By RebabTime.

 You can still be a good friend and say "No". Sometimes we need to balance our desire to care for others with our own personal needs. Don't give yourself away!...By Lynda Fields. I don't need you just to be honest with me, I need you to be loyal to me. Being honest doesn't make you faithful, loyalty does. Telling the truth doesn't make you a good person, it just doesn't make you a liar. A loyal heart doesn't put itself in a position to have to tell the truth about living a lie. I'll always respect an honest person, but I'll only trust a loyal one…By #RehabTime. It is not your job to like me…It's mine…By Byron Katie.

"My belief in social justice means that I believe in equality, in the dignity and value of all human lives. It means that sometimes not everything is about you. It means that sometimes, you need to have a seat and listen"…By Michelle Denise Jackson. There's a difference between knowing somebody and hearing about somebody. Just because you heard, doesn't mean you know…By Trent Shelton.

PEOPLE ARE CONFUSED ABOUT FORGIVENESS; IT'S NOT ABOUT EXCUSING SOMEONE'S ACTIONS…IT'S ABOUT NOT ALLOWING THEIR ACTIONS TO HURT YOU ANYMORE…BY SUE FITZMAURICE. STOP COMPARING YOURSELF TO OTHERS, YOU HAVE YOUR OWN RACE TO RUN. FINISH WELL….BY DR JAMES MAKAMBA.

THE SERVICE YOU DO FOR OTHERS IS THE RENT YOU PAY FOR YOUR ROOM HERE ON EARTH…BY MUHAMMAD ALI. PEOPLE WHO JUDGE YOU BY YOUR PAST, DON'T BELONG IN YOUR PRESENT…BY MANDY HALE.

BE CAREFUL WHO YOU TRUST, IF SOMEONE WILL DISCUSS OTHERS WITH YOU, THEY WILL CERTAINLY DISCUSS YOU WITH OTHERS…BY

BAISDEN LIVE. DON'T TELL ME HOW TO BE ME WHEN YOU CAN'T EVEN FIGURE YOURSELF OUT...BY BAISDEN LIVE.

SOMETIMES THE PERSON WHO TRIES TO KEEP EVERYONE HAPPY IS ALWAYS THE MOST LONELY PERSON. SO NEVER LEAVE THEM ALONE BECAUSE THEY WILL NEVER SAY THAT THEY NEED YOU...BY QUOTESBUDDY.COM. PRACTISING FORGIVENESS DOES NOT MEAN ACCEPTING WRONG DOING...BY DALAI LAMA.

WHEN YOU BEGIN TO ATTRACT PEOPLE WHO SUPPORT YOU, YOUR DREAMS ARE BEGINNING TO UNFOLD...BY SUE FITZMAURICE. I LIKE RUMOURS, I FIND OUT SO MUCH ABOUT ME THAT I DIDN'T EVEN KNOW...UNKNOWN. WHENEVER I FEEL WEAK, I'LL REMEMBER THOSE WHO MAKE ME STRONG AND WHENEVER I START TO DOUBT MYSELF, I'LL REMEMBER THOSE WHO BELIEVE IN ME...BY TIA MOWRY. WE CANNOT TEACH PEOPLE ANYTHING; WE CAN ONLY HELP THEM DISCOVER IT WITHIN THEMSELVES...BY GALILEO GALILEI. SUCCESSFUL PEOPLE BUILD EACH OTHER UP, THEY MOTIVATE, INSPIRE AND PUSH EACH OTHER. UNSUCCESSFUL PEOPLE JUST HATE, BLAME AND COMPLAIN...BY VICKI YOHE. FAKE PEOPLE DON'T SURPRISE ME ANYMORE, LOYAL PEOPLE DO...BY PHUCKYQUOTE.

LET US NOT FORGET THAT IT IS FRIENDSHIP, ALWAYS FRIENDSHIP, THAT IS THE GREAT SOURCE AND WELL SPRING OF FUN IN OUT LIVES...BY BRENDON BURCHARD. KNOWING A PERSON IS LIKE MUSIC, WHAT ATTRACTS US TO THEM IS THEIR MELODY, 'N AS WE GET TO KNOW WHO THEY ARE, WE LEARN THEIR LYRICS...BY THE NATIONAL R&B MUSIC SOCIETY INC. DON'T CHASE PEOPLE, BE YOURSELF, DO YOUR OWN THING, AND WORK HARD. THE RIGHT PEOPLE...THE ONES WHO REALLY BELONG IN YOUR LIFE WILL COME TO YOU AND STAY...BY WILL SMITH. BETTER BE SLAPPED WITH THE TRUTH, THAN KISSED WITH A LIE...A RUSSIAN PROVERB. I HATE IT WHEN YOU HAVE TO BE NICE TO SOMEONE YOU REALLY WANT TO THROW A BRICK AT...BY FIFE AND DAVE. DON'T LET THE BEHAVIOUR OF OTHERS DESTROY

YOUR INNER PEACE...BY DALAI LAMA. DO NOT GET UPSET WITH PEOPLE OR SITUATIONS, BOTH ARE POWERLESS WITHOUT YOUR REACTION...BY VINCENT HAPPY MNISI.

GRADES DON'T MEASURE INTELLIGENCE AND AGE DOESN'T DEFINE MATURITY...BY        SILENCE IS BETTER THAN BULLSHIT...BY THE PROGRESSIVE RADIO NETWORK. MY HAPPINESS DOES NOT DEPEND UPON ANYONE ELSE'S...BY LYNDA FIELDS.COM.

I DON'T NEED OTHER PEOPLE TO HAVE AN OPEN MIND FOR ME TO BE HAPPY. I'M THE ONLY ONE WHO NEEDS AN OPEN MIND...BY BYRON KATIE. I NO LONGER HAVE THE ENERGY FOR MEANINGLESS FRIENDSHIP,      FORCED      INTERACTIONS,      OR      UNNECESSARY CONVERSATIONS...BY BASIDEN LIVE. YOU CAN ALWAYS COUNT ON ME TO BE THE ASS-HOLE WHO GIVES YOU A REALITY CHECK INSTEAD OF TELLING YOU WHAT YOU WANT TO HEAR...BY YOUR.E.CARDS.

I PROMISE MYSELF...TO MAKE ALL MY FRIENDS FEEL THAT THERE IS SOMETHING WORTHWHILE IN THEM...BY CHRISTIAN D. LARSON. YOU ARE IN CHARGE OF HOW YOU REACT TO THE PEOPLE AND EVENTS IN YOUR LIFE. YOU CAN EITHER GIVE NEGATIVITY POWER OVER YOUR LIFE OR YOU CAN CHOOSE HAPPINESS INSTEAD...BY ANAIS NIN. DON'T ALLOW ANYONE TO TAKE YOU FOR GRANTED YOU ARE TOO VALUABLE TO NOT BE APPRECIATED...BY VICKI YOHE.

SOME PEOPLE DON'T KNOW HOW TO APPRECIATE A FRIEND BECAUSE THEY DON'T KNOW HOW TO BE ONE...BY DR FARRAH GRAY. FRIENDSHIP IS NOT A COLLECTION OF A MESSAGE...IT IS A COLLECTION OF HEARTS...ALL FRIENDS ARE NOT TRUE...BUT TRUE FRIENDS ARE VERY FEW...BY LAUGHING COLOURS. DO WHAT YOU CAN TO HELP PEOPLE BUT HAVE THE WISDOM TO ACCEPT YOUR LIMITS...BY BRYANT MCGILL. BE MINDFUL OF WHERE YOU PLEDGE YOUR ALLEGIANCE SOMETIMES IT'S HARD TO TELL FRIEND FROM FOE...BY ANNA PEREIRA. REMEMBER THAT GUYS THAT GAVE UP? NEITHER DOES ANYBODY ELSE BY BASIDEN LIVE.

YOU CANNOT SAVE EVERYONE. SOME PEOPLE ARE GOING TO DESTROY THEMSELVES NO MATTER HOW MUCH YOU TRY TO HELP THEM...BY BRYAN MCGILL. LIFE IS TOO SHORT TO WAKE UP IN THE MORNING WITH REGRETS. SO LOVE THE PEOPLE WHO TREAT YOU RIGHT, FORGIVE THE ONES WHO DON'T AND BELIEVE EVERYTHING HAPPENS FOR A REASON...BY FORTUNATE YOUTH. MINDING YOUR OWN BUSINESS GOES FAR BEYOND SIMPLY AVOIDING THE TEMPTATION TO TRY AND SOLVE OTHER PEOPLE'S PROBLEMS. IT ALSO INCLUDES EAVESDROPPING; GOSSIPING; TALKING BEHIND OTHER PEOPLE'S BACKS AND ANALYSING OR TRYING TO FIGURE OUT OTHER PEOPLE. ONE OF THE MAJOR REASONS MOST OF US FOCUS ON THE SHORT COMINGS OR PROBLEMS OF OTHERS IS TO AVOID LOOKING AT OURSELVES...BY RICHARD CARLSON.

WHEN YOU HOLD RESENTMENT TOWARDS ANOTHER, YOU ARE BOUND TO THAT PERSON OR CONDITION BY AN EMOTIONAL LINK THAT IS STRONGER THAN STEEL. FORGIVENESS IS THE ONLY WAY TO DISSOLVE THAT LINK AND GET FREE...BY CATHERINE PONDER. ALWAYS HELP SOMEONE. YOU MIGHT BE THE ONLY ONE WHO DOES...BY MELISSA HART.

WHEN OTHER PEOPLE TREAT YOU POORLY, WALK AWAY, SMILE AND KEEP BEING YOU. DON'T EVER LET SOMEONE ELSE'S BITTERNESS CHANGE THE PERSON YOU ARE...BY MARCANDANGLES.COM. SOME PEOPLE DON'T LIKE YOU BECAUSE YOUR STRENGTH REMINDS THEM OF THEIR WEAKNESS. DON'T LET THEIR HATE SLOW YOU DOWN...BY THEMA DAVIS.

THE MOMENT YOU FEEL LIKE YOU HAVE TO PROVE YOUR WORTH TO SOMEONE IS THE MOMENT TO ABSOLUTELY AND UTTERLY WALK AWAY...BY ALYSIA HARRIS.

YOUR JOB ISN'T TO JUDGE. YOUR JOB ISN'T TO FIGURE OUT IF SOMEONE DESERVES SOMETHING OR DECIDE WHO IS RIGHT OR WRONG. YOUR JOB

IS TO LIFT THE FALLEN, RESTORE THE BROKEN AND HEAL THE HURTING...BY JOEL OSTEEN.

WE ARE ALL EQUAL-WHETHER ONE IS RICH OR POOR, EDUCATED OR ILLITERATE; RELIGIOUS OR NONE BELIEVING, MAN OR WOMAN; BLACK, WHITE OR BROWN WE ALL THE SAME. PHYSICALLY, EMOTIONALLY AND MENTALLY WE ARE ALL EQUAL. WE ALL SHARE BASIC NEEDS FOR FOOD; SHELTER; SAFETY AND LOVE. WE ALL ASPIRE TO HAPPINESS AND WE ALL SHUN SUFFERING. EACH OF US HAS HOPES, WORRIES, FEARS AND DREAMS. EACH OF US WANTS THE BEST FOR OUR FAMILY AND LOVED ONES. WE ALL EXPERIENCE PAIN WHEN WE SUFFER LOSS AND JOY WHEN WE ACHIEVE WHAT WE SEEK. ON THIS FUNDAMENTAL LEVEL, RELIGION, ETHNICITY, CULTURE AND LANGUAGE MAKES NO DIFFERENCE...BY THE DALAI LAMA

NOT EVERY PERSON IS GOING TO UNDERSTAND YOU AND THAT'S OKAY. THEY HAVE A RIGHT TO THEIR OPINION AND YOU HAVE EVERY RIGHT TO IGNORE IT...BY JOEL OSTEEN. BE YOU NOT MATTER WHAT...BY VINCENT HAPPY MNISI. THE IDEA IS NOT TO SEE THROUGH ONE ANOTHER, BUT TO SEE ONE ANOTHER THROUGH...BY C. D. JACKSON. BE OPEN TO OTHERS; GIVE PEOPLE A CHANCE. BE OPEN TO YOURSELF; GIVE YOURSELF A CHANCE...BY BRYANT MCGILL. THE KEY IS TO KEEP COMPANY ONLY WITH PEOPLE WHO UPLIFT YOU, WHOSE PRESENCE CALLS FORTH YOUR BEST...BRYANT MCGILL. THE WHOLE WORLD CAN LOVE YOU, BUT THAT LOVE WILL NOT MAKE YOU HAPPY. WHAT WILL MAKE YOU HAPPY IS THE LOVE COMING OUT OF YOU...BY DON MIGUEL RUIZ. THE BOOK OF FORGIVING: LIVING IN PEACE WITH OTHERS REQUIRES HAVING PEACE AND HARMONY WITHIN OURSELVES...BY DESMOND TUTU AND MPHO TUTU.

THE MOST BEAUTIFUL PEOPLE WE HAVE KNOWN ARE THOSE WHO HAVE KNOWN DEFEAT, KNOWN SUFFERING, KNOWN STRUGGLE, KNOWN LOSS, AND HAVE FOUND THEIR WAY OUT OF THE DEPTHS. THESE PEOPLE HAVE AN APPRECIATION A SENSITIVITY, AND AN UNDERSTANDING OF LIFE THAT FILLS THEM WITH COMPASSION, GENTLENESS AND A DEEP LOVING CONCERN. BEAUTIFUL PEOPLE DO NOT JUST HAPPEN...BY SOUL VISION HEALING.

BE KIND, GENTLE AND LOVING TOWARDS EVERYONE YOU MEET. WHEN I OFFER LOVING KINDNESS TO OTHERS SOMETHING HAPPENS TO MY OWN HEART. I FEEL IT RIGHT THERE INSIDE OF ME. EACH TIME I EXTEND LOVE...I FEEL MY SPIRIT GROWING CLOSER TO THE TRUTH...BY EILEEN DIELESSEN. BEING CONSIDERED CRAZY BY THOSE WHO ARE STILL VICTIMS OF CULTURAL CONDITIONING IS A COMPLIMENT...BY JASON HAIRSTON. WHO EVER LAUGHS AT YOUR DREAMS DOES NOT HAVE THE COURAGE TO FOLLOW THEIR OWN...BY ANNA PEREIRA.

FORGIVENESS DOESN'T MEAN TRUST SOMEONE AGAIN. FORGIVENESS DOESN'T MEAN PUT YOURSELF IN HARMS WAY AGAIN. FORGIVENESS DOESN'T MEAN JUSTICE IS SERVED. FORGIVENESS MEANS YOU GET YOUR FREEDOM BACK...BY PROJECT-FORGIVE.COM.

DO SOMETHING WONDERFUL, PEOPLE MAY IMITATE IT...BY BRAIN TRACY.COM. STOP GETTING ATTACHED TO PEOPLE SO FAST, BECAUSE ATTACHMENTS LEAD TO EXPECTATIONS AND EXPECTATIONS LEADS TO DISAPPOINTMENTS...BY KILLIAN F. BUKUTU. IF YOU ARE WHO YOU ARE IT IS REALLY HARD TO STEAL...BY IGGU POP AND BEFORE YOU DIAGNOSE YOURSELF WITH DEPRESSION OR LOW SELF ESTEEM, FIRST MAKE SURE THAT YOU ARE NOT IN FACT, SURROUNDED BY ASS-HOLES...SIGMUND FREUD.

WE WOULD DO OURSELVES A TREMENDOUS FAVOUR BY LETTING GO OF THE PEOPLE WHO POISON OUR SPIRIT...BY ANGIE KARANKREZOS.

SOMETIMES YOU HAVE TO ACCEPT THE TRUTH AND STOP WASTING PRECIOUS TIME ON THE WRONG PEOPLE...BY DR FARRAH GRAY. FOOLS TAKE A KNIFE AND STAB PEOPLE IN THE BACK. THE WISE TAKE A KNIFE, CUT THE CORD AND FREE THEMSELVES FROM THE FOOLS...UNKNOWN. SOME PEOPLE ARE SO ADDICTED TO THEIR MISERY THAT THEY WILL DESTROY ANYTHING THAT GETS IN THE WAY OF THEIR FIX...BY BRYANT MCGILL. NO MAN OR WOMAN IS AN ISLAND. ASK FOR HELP, FOR WHAT YOU NEED...BY SUE FITZMAURICE.

EVERYONE HAS THEIR OWN PATH. WALK YOURS WITH INTEGRITY AND WISH ALL OTHERS PEACE ON THEIR JOURNEY. WHEN YOUR PATHS MERGE, REJOICE FOR THEIR PRESENCE IN YOUR LIFE. WHEN THE PATHS ARE SEPARATED, RETURN TO THE WHOLENESS OF YOURSELF, GIVE THANKS FOR THE FOOTPRINTS LEFT ON YOUR SOUL, AND EMBRACE THE TIME TO JOURNEY ON YOUR OWN...UNKNOWN.

SOMETIMES A PERSON NEEDS US TO ABANDON THEM, BUT WE HANG ON ANYWAY, WHICH CAN BE DEVASTATING FOR BOTH PARTIES. HELPING OTHERS CAN SOMETIMES EVEN BE A CONVENIENT DISTRACTION FROM ADDRESSING OUR OWN UNRESOLVED ISSUES. WHEN SOMEONE YOU KNOW IS SO TOXIC AND DESTRUCTIVE, THAT THEY ARE POISONING YOUR LIFE, YOU HAVE TO CREATE SOME DISTANCE. THEY NEED YOU TO WALK AWAY AS MUCH AS YOU NEED IT...BY BRYANT MCGILL.

IF PEOPLE SAY SOMETHING BAD ABOUT YOU, JUDGE YOU AS IF THEY KNOW YOU...DON'T GET AFFECTED...REMEMBER THIS DOGS BARK IF THEY DON'T KNOW THE PERSON...BY HUSHWORLD. YOU TEACH OTHER PEOPLE YOU SPEND THE MOST TIME WITH CHOOSE WISELY...BY BAISDEN LIVE. YOU BECOME LIKE THE PEOPLE YOU SPEND THE MOST TIME WITH CHOOSE WISELY...BY BAISDEN LIVE.

IF YOU MUST LOSE FAITH IN HUMANITY. HUMANITY IS AN OCEAN; IF A FEW DROPS OF THE OCEAN ARE DIRTY, THE OCEAN DOES NOT BECOME

DIRTY...BY GANDHI. LIVE YOUR LIFE IN EVERY WAY TO EARN AND KEEP THE RESPECT OF THE PEOPLE YOU RESPECT...BY BRIAN TRACY.

WHAT DID YOU LEARN YESTERDAY? AND MORE IMPORTANTLY, WHAT DID YOU TEACH TO SOMEONE ELSE YESTERDAY? WHAT YOU GIVE AWAY WILL MULTIPLY IN YOUR LIFE...BY BISHOP DALE C. BRONNER. I HAVE LEARNED...THAT IT IS NOT WHAT I HAVE IN MY LIFE BUT WHO I HAVE IN MY LIFE THAT COUNTS...BY MICHAEL BAISDEN.

YOU PRACTICE FORGIVENESS: TO LET OTHERS KNOW THAT YOU NO LONGER WISH TO BE IN A STATE OF HOSTILITY WITH THEM AND TO FREE YOURSELF FROM THE SELF-DEFEATING ENERGY OF RESENTMENT. SEND LOVE IN SOME FORM TO THOSE YOU FEEL HAVE WRONGED YOU AND NOTICE HOW MUCH BETTER YOU FEEL...BY WAYNE DYER.

FINDING YOUR PASSION ISN'T JUST ABOUT CAREERS AND MONEY. IT'S ABOUT FINDING YOUR AUTHENTIC SELF. THE ONE YOU'VE BURIED BENEATH OTHER PEOPLE'S NEEDS...BY KRISTIN HANNAH. NOT EVERYONE WILL SHARE YOUR VISION. THAT STILL DOES NOT MEAN THAT THERE IS SOMETHING WRONG WITH YOUR SIGHT...BY SUE KREBS

AS LONG AS YOU CAN SWEETEN ANOTHER'S PAIN, LIFE IS NOT IN VAIN...BY HELEN KELLER. JUST BEING THERE FOR SOMEONE CAN SOMETIMES BRING HOPE WHEN ALL SEEMS HOPELESS...BY DAVE G. L. LEWELLYN. HOLD YOURSELF RESPONSIBLE FOR A HIGHER STANDARD THAN ANYBODY ELSE EXPECTS OF YOU. NEVER EXCUSE YOURSELF. NEVER PITY YOURSELF. BE A HARD MASTER TO YOURSELF AND LENIENT TO EVERYBODY ELSE...BY HENRY WARD BEECHER. I HAVE LEARNED...THAT IT'S NOT WHAT I HAVE IN MY LIFE BUT WHO I HAVE IN MY LIFE THAT COUNTS...BY MICHAEL BAISDEN.

IF SOMEONE HAS OFFENDED YOU, INSULTED YOU, OR DISAPPOINTED YOU, LET IT GO! IF YOU ARE REMEMBERING ALL THE WAYS YOU HAVE BEEN HURT OR FORGOTTEN, LET IT GO! ASK YOURSELF? WHAT GOOD

DOES IT DO FOR ME TO HOLD ON TO THIS...UNKNOWN. THERE IS A NOBILITY IN COMPASSION, A BEAUTY IN EMPATHY, A GRACE IN FORGIVENESS...BY JOHN CONNOLLY.

BLESSED ARE THOSE WHO CAN GIVE WITHOUT REMEMBERING AND TAKE WITHOUT FORGETTING. SOME OF THE MOST AMAZING PEOPLE IN THE WORLD WERE NOT PERFECT; THEY WERE SCARRED BY SUFFERING, HARDSHIP, LOSSES AND IMPERFECTIONS. BUT WHEN THEY RECOVERED THEY WERE STRONGER, WISER AND MORE LOVING AND COMPASSIONATE. YOUR LIFE IS GOING TO GET BETTER IN THE PROPER TIME, AND YOU WILL BE STRONGER AND MORE AT PEACE THAN EVER BEFORE...BY BRYANT MCGILL.

MOVE ON TO THE GOOD STUFF...IF YOU HAVE A BITE OF SOMETHING NASTY, YOU LEAVE IT AND NIBBLE ON THE OTHER STUFF THAT TASTES GOOD RIGHT? SO WHEN SOMEONE HAS A NEGATIVE THING TO SAY BRUSH IT OFF MOVE ON, DON'T CHEW ON IT...SPIT IT OUT! SAY "THANK YOU", ENJOY AND APPRECIATE THE NICE THINGS THAT ARE SAID TO YOU. COMPLIMENTS TASTE MUCH BETTER...BY ANNA PEREIRA.

YOU CAN'T PLEASE EVERYBODY. THE BEST YOU CAN DO, IS THE BEST YOU CAN DO. IF A PERSON CAN'T APPRECIATE YOUR BEST EFFORT THAT'S THEIR PERSONAL PROBLEM. BE OKAY WITH THAT!...BY TONY GASKINS. NO TIME IS BETTER SPENT THAN IN THE SERVICE OF OTHERS...BY BRYANT MCGILL. DON'T TAKE ME FOR GRANTED BECAUSE UNLIKE OTHERS I AM NOT AFRAID TO WALK AWAY...BY STEVEN AITCHISON.

WE JUDGE PEOPLE TODAY BY THEY ACTIONS...WE DON'T KNOW THAT ACTIONS ON THE OUTSIDE CAN BE DIFFERENT TO ACTIONS ON THE INSIDE. BECAUSE OF THIS WE DON'T KNOW OUR FRIENDS AND OUR

ENEMIES...BY T. B. JOSHUA. KNOW YOUR WORTHINESS, KNOW WHEN YOU HAVE HAD ENOUGH OF SOMETHING'S. AND KEEP MOVING FROM PEOPLE WHO RUIN YOUR HAPPINESS...BY VINCENT HAPPY MNISI.

YOU DON'T EVER HAVE TO FEEL GUILTY ABOUT REMOVING TOXIC PEOPLE FROM YOUR LIFE. IT DOESN'T MATTER WHETHER SOMEONE IS A RELATIVE, ROMANTIC INTEREST, EMPLOYER, CHILDHOOD FRIEND OR A NEW ACQUAINTANCE...YOU DON'T HAVE TO MAKE ROOM FOR PEOPLE WHO CAUSE YOU PAIN OR MAKE YOU FEEL SMALL. IT'S ONE THING IF A PERSON OWNS UP TO THEIR BEHAVIOUR AND MAKES AN EFFORT TO CHANGE. BUT IF A PERSON DISREGARDS YOUR FEELINGS, IGNORES YOUR BOUNDARIES, AND CONTINUES TO TREAT YOU IN A HARMFUL WAY, THEY NEED TO GO...BY DANIELL KOEPKE.

A MAN WHO ISOLATES HIMSELF SEEKS HIS OWN DESIRE; HE RAGES AGAINST ALL WISE JUDGEMENT...A FOOL HAS NO DELIGHT IN UNDERSTANDING BUT IN EXPRESSING HIS OWN HEART...PROVERBS 18 V 1&2. "THERE PERSON YOU TOOK FOR GRANTED TODAY, MAY TURN OUT TO BE THE PERSON YOU NEED TOMORROW, BE CAREFUL ON HOW YOU TREAT PEOPLE...SOME PEOPLE CREATE THEIR OWN STORMS, THEN GET UPSET WHEN IT RAINS" BY BAISDEN LIVE

DO WHAT IS RIGHT FOR YOU. NO ONE ELSE IS WALKING IN YOUR SHOES...BY LYNDA FIELDS. NEVER BLAME ANYONE IN YOUR LIFE. GOOD PEOPLE GIVE YOU HAPPINESS, BAD PEOPLE GIVE YOU EXPERIENCE. WORST PEOPLE GIVE YOU A LESSON AND BEST PEOPLE GIVE YOU MEMORIES...BY POWER OF POSITIVITY.COM.

TRY NOT TO TAKE THINGS PERSONALLY, WHAT PEOPLE SAY ABOUT YOU IS A REFLECTION OF THEM, NOT YOU...BY PINOY RAP RADIO. DON'T LET ANYONE ELSE'S FEARS, LIMITATIONS OR SENSE OF LACK DETERMINE HOW YOU LIVE YOUR LIFE...BY SUE KREBS. YOU CAN'T LET PEOPLE SCARE YOU. YOU CAN'T GO YOUR WHOLE LIFE TRYING TO

PLEASE EVERYONE ELSE. YOU CAN'T GO THROUGH LIFE WORRIED ABOUT WHAT EVERYONE ELSE IS GOING TO THINK. WHETHER IT'S YOUR HAIR, CLOTHES, WHAT EVER YOU HAVE TO SAY, HOW YOU FEEL, WHAT YOU BELIEVE AND WHAT YOU HAVE. YOU CAN'T LET THE JUDGEMENT OF OTHERS STOP YOU FROM BEING YOU. BECAUSE IF YOU DO, YOU'RE NO LONGER YOU, YOU'RE SOMEONE EVERYONE ELSE WANTS YOU TO BE...UNKNOWN. SEEKING THE APPROVAL OF OTHERS WILL NEVER BRING YOU HAPPINESS. YOU DON'T NEED ANYBODIES PERMISSION, YOU HAVE TO TRUST IN YOUR OWN VALUE IF YOU WANT OTHERS TO RECOGNISE YOUR VALUE...BY BRYANT MCGILL.

WHEN SOMEONE IS VICIOUS TOWARDS YOU THEY ARE GIVING YOU A GLIMPSE OF THE PAIN THEY ARE CARRYING IN THEMSELVES...BY BRYANT MCGILL. A HOT TEMPERED MAN STIRS UP DISSENSION, BUT A PATIENT MAN CALMS A QUARREL...PROVERBS 15 V 18. ATTRACT WHAT YOU EXPECT, REFLECT WHAT YOU DESIRE, BECOME WHAT YOU EXPECT, MIRROR WHAT YOU ADMIRE...BY NICOLE STEPHENS. SOME PEOPLE ARE GOING TO REJECT YOU, SIMPLY BECAUSE YOU SHINE TOO BRIGHT FOR THEM. AND THAT'S OKAY. KEEP SHINING...BY SIMPLYBHANGRA.COM.

I AM ONLY RESPONSIBLE FOR WHAT I SAY...NOT FOR WHAT YOU UNDERSTAND...BY ZEN-SATIONAL LIVING. THE OLDER I GET, THE LESS I CARE ABOUT WHAT PEOPLE THINK OF ME. THEREFORE THE OLDER I GET, THE MORE I ENJOY LIFE...BY BAISDEN LIVE. I AM NOT A PERFECT PERSON. I MAKE A LOT OF MISTAKES. BUT I REALLY APPRECIATE THOSE PEOPLE WHO STAY WITH ME AFTER KNOWING HOW I REALLY AM...BY STEVEN AITCHISONS.

SOMETIMES A PERSON NEEDS US TO ABANDON THEM, BUT WE HANG ON ANYWAY, WHICH CAN BE DEVASTATING FOR BOTH PARTIES. HELPING OTHERS CAN SOMETIMES EVEN BE A CONVENIENT DISTRACTION FROM ADDRESSING OUT OWN UNRESOLVED ISSUES WHEN SOMEONE YOU KNOW IS SO TOXIC AND DESTRUCTIVE THAT THEY ARE

POISONING YOUR LIFE, YOU HAVE TO TO CREATE SOME DISTANCE. THEY NEED YOU TO WALK AWAY AS MUCH AS YOU NEED IT...BY BRYANT MCGILL.

DO WHAT YOU CAN TO HELP PEOPLE BUT HAVE THE WISDOM TO KNOW YOUR LIMITS...BY BRYANT MCGILL. YOU CAN'T MAKE SOMEONE BECOME SOMETHING THEY AREN'T READY TO BE. IF THEY WON'T GROW WITH YOU, BE WILLING TO GROW WITHOUT THEM...BY TONY GASKINS.

AS SOON AS I STOP COMPARING MYSELF WITH OTHERS. I AM FREE TO ENJOY BEING ME...BY LYNDA FIELDS. OPEN MINDED PEOPLE DO NOT FEEL THE NEED TO IMPOSE THEIR BELIEFS. CLOSED MINDED PEOPLE BELIEVE IT'S THEIR WAY OR IT'S THE WRONG WAY. WHICH ARE YOU?...BY STEVEN AITCHISON. THE SIGN OF A BEAUTIFUL PERSON IS THAT THEY ALWAYS SEE BEAUTY IN OTHERS...BY SUE FITZMAURICE.

LEARN TO BE ALONE AND TO LIKE IT. THERE IS NOTHING MORE FREEING AND EMPOWERING THAN LEARNING TO LIKE YOUR OWN COMPANY...BY MENTORS CHANNEL. SOMETIMES WALKING AWAY HAS NOTHING TO DO WITH WEAKNESS, AND EVERYTHING TO DO WITH STRENGTH. WE WALK AWAY NOT BECAUSE WE WANT OTHERS TO REALISE OUR VALUE AND WORTH. BUT BECAUSE WE FINALLY REALISE OUR OWN WORTHINESS...UNKNOWN. EVERYTHING YOU SAY TO SOMEONE ELSE IS FOR YOUR CLARITY NOT THEIRS...YOU ARE PRESENTING YOURSELF, TO YOURSELF, FOR YOURSELF AT EVERY MOMENT...BY BRYANT MCGILL. NEVER CONFUSE EDUCATION WITH INTELLIGENCE...BY COLLECTIVE EVOLUTION.

IT'S NOT THE COLOUR OF OUR SKIN THAT MAKES US DIFFERENT, IT'S THE COLOUR OF OF OUR THOUGHTS...BY STEVEN AITCHISON. NEVER UNDERESTIMATE THE POWER OF STUPID PEOPLE IN LARGE GROUPS...BY HUMOR PAGE. BE KIND, FOR EVERYONE YOU MEET IS FIGHTING A BATTLE YOU KNOW NOTHING ABOUT...WENDY MASS. SOME PEOPLE ARE LIKE CLOUDS, WHEN THEY GO IT'S A BEAUTIFUL DAY...BY

BE HAPPY&AWESOME. A NEGATIVE THINKERS SEES DIFFICULTY IN EVERY OPPORTUNITY, A POSITIVE THINKER SEES AN OPPORTUNITY IN EVERY DIFFICULTY. RULES ARE FOR PEOPLE WHO DON'T KNOW WHAT TO DO. THINK FOR YOURSELF QUESTION EVERYTHING?. LIVE IN SUCH A WAY THAT IF SOMEONE SPOKE BADLY OF YOU, NO ONE WOULD BELIEVE IT...BY...VINCENT HAPPY MNISI. IN LIFE, SOMETIMES GETTING HURT IS A NECESSARY PATH, DO NOT DENY YOURSELF OF THIS EXPERIENCE, BUT NEVER DWELL IN IT. YOU HAVE TO GO THROUGH IT AND NOT AROUND IT FOR YOU TO GET OVER IT. BY DODINSKY .COM.

I GAVE MY ALL STILL THEY SAID IT WASN'T ENOUGH. I TRIED TO DO BETTER STILL THEY MAGNIFIED MY FLAWS. I PUT OTHERS BEFORE ME STILL THEY SAID I WAS SELFISH. I SHOWED THEM MY HEART STILL THEY ONLY SAW MY PAST. I SHARED MY STORY. STILL THEY RIDICULED MY MISTAKES. I TOLD THEM MY DREAMS STILL THEY LAUGHED AT MY VISIONS. I GAVE MY LIFE TO CHRIST STILL THEY POINTED OUT MY SINS. BUT THROUGH IT ALL I'VE REALISED...I'M HERE TO PLEASE GOD NOT THEM...BY TRENT SHELTON.

OUR LIVES ARE STORYBOOKS THAT WE WRITE FOR OURSELVES; WONDERFULLY ILLUSTRATED BY THE PEOPLE WE MEET...UNKNOWN. DON'T STAY WHERE YOU ARE TOLERATED, GO WHERE YOU ARE CELEBRATED...BY WAKE UP WORLD.

LEARN HOW TO SAY NO! DON'T LET YOUR MOUTH OVERLOAD YOUR BACK...BY JIM ROHN. YOU'LL END UP REAL DISAPPOINTED IF YOU THINK PEOPLE WILL DO FOR YOU AS YOU DO FOR THEM. NOT EVERYONE HAS THE SAME HEART AS YOU...BY KILLIAN F. BUKUTU.

MAKE YOUR LIFESTYLE A LIVING TESTAMENT FOR OTHERS TO SEE AND HOPE TO LIVE LIKE YOU...OUR LIFESTYLES SHOULD BE A LIVING TESTAMENT FOR ALL TO SEE AND HOPE TO BE LIKE YOU!...BY VINCENT HAPPY MNISI. THE LORD SHALL PRESERVE YOUR GOING OUT AND COMING IN FROM THIS TIME FORTH AND EVEN FOR EVERMORE... PSALM 12V 8. IT TAKES STRENGTH TO NOT GET OFFENDED BY THE

OPINIONS OF OTHERS. SELF CONFIDENCE AND SELF WORTH CREATE THE FOUNDATION OF THAT STRENGTH...BY ANNA PEREIRA.

FORGIVE THE PAST. IT IS OVER, LEARN FROM IT AND LET GO. PEOPLE ARE CONSTANTLY CHANGING AND GROWING. DON'T CLING TO A LIMITED, DISCONNECTED NEGATIVE IMAGES OF A PERSON IN THE PAST. SEE THAT PERSON NOW. YOUR RELATIONSHIP IS ALWAYS ALIVE AND CHANGING...BY BRAIN WEISS.

PEOPLE INSPIRE YOU OR THEY DRAIN YOU PICK THEM WISELY...BY HANS F. HANSEN. THE LESS YOU RESPOND, CRITICAL, ARGUMENTATIVE PEOPLE, THE MORE PEACEFUL YOUR LIFE WILL BECOME...BY MANDY HALE. THE GENERAL POPULATION DOESN'T KNOW WHAT'S HAPPENING. AND IT DOESN'T EVEN KNOW THAT IT DOESN'T KNOW...BY. DON'T TRY TO FIGURE OUT WHAT OTHER PEOPLE WANT TO HEAR FROM YOU; FIGURE OUT WHAT YOU HAVE TO SAY IT'S THE ONE AND ONLY THING YOU HAVE TO OFFER...BARBARA KINGSOLVER. I HAVE COME TO REALISE THAT THE ONLY PEOPLE I NEED IN MY LIFE ARE THE ONES WHO NEED ME IN THEIRS EVEN WHEN I HAVE NOTHING ELSE TO OFFER BUT MYSELF...UNKNOWN.

IT'S NOT ABOUT WHO IS REAL TO YOUR FACE, IT;S ABOUT WHO STAYS REAL BEHIND YOUR BACK...BY BAISDEN LIVE. SOME PEOPLE WILL ONLY LOVE YOU AS MUCH AS THEY CAN USE YOU...LOYALTY ENDS WHERE THE BENEFITS STOP...BY BAISDEN LIVE.

SURROUND YOURSELF WITH THOSE ON THE SAME MISSION AS YOU IF THE PEOPLE YOU SURROUND YOURSELF WITH AREN'T GOING YOUR WAY...DROP THEM OFF WHERE THEY'RE GOING AND KEEP MOVING FULL SPEED AHEAD...BY MIKE EPPS. I LOVE PEOPLE WHO MAKE ME LAUGH, I HONESTLY THINK IT'S THE THING LIKE MOST TO LAUGH. IT CURES A MULTITUDE OF ILLS. IT'S PROBABLY THE MOST IMPORTANT THING IN A PERSON...BY AUDREY HEPBURN.

EVERYONE IS A TEACHER. SOME I SEEK, SOME I SUBCONSCIOUSLY ATTRACT. OFTEN I LEARN SIMPLY BY OBSERVING OTHERS. SOME MAYBE COMPLETELY UNAWARE THAT I AM LEARNING FROM THEM, YET I BOW DEEPLY IN GRATITUDE...BY SPIRIT SCIENCE.

THEY SEE THE SHINE, NOT THE GRIND. THEY SEE THE PRAISE, NOT THE PAIN. THEY THE MONEY, NOT THE WORK. THEY THINK IT'S EASY, NOT STRESSFUL. THEY THINK IT'S A CAREER, NOT A CALLING. THEY THINK I CHOSE IT, NOT THAT IT CHOSE ME LORD, IF THEY ONLY KNEW...BY TONY GASKINS. SOMETIMES IT'S BETTER TO POLITELY EXCUSE YOURSELF FROM A PERSON IGNORANCE THAN ENTERTAIN THEM WITH YOUR INTELLIGENCE...BY DR FARRAH GRAY. DON'T TRY TO FIGURE OUT WHAT OTHER PEOPLE WANT TO HEAR FROM YOU; FIGURE OUT WHAT YOU HAVE TO SAY. IT;S THE ONE AND ONLY THING YOU HAVE TO OFFER...BY BARBARA KINGSOLVER.

DISAPPOINTMENT IS COMING, FOR SURE! PEOPLE ARE GOING TO HURT YOU IN WAYS YOU WOULD NEVER HAVE BELIEVED EVEN POSSIBLE. YOU ARE GOING TO BE LET DOWN AND DEEPLY BETRAYED. AND THERE IS ONLY ONE THING TO DO WHEN YOU ARE TRAGICALLY LET DOWN. LET GO! NO MATTER HOW WRONG THEY WERE, HOLDING ON WILL NOT MAKE IT RIGHT, AND IT WILL EAT YOU ALIVE OVER TIME. DON'T LET THEM KILL YOU TWICE. LETTING GO IS THE ONLY WAY...BY BRYANT MCGILL.

YOU'RE ELEVATED BY OTHERS WHO BELIEVE IN YOU!...BY BOB BEAUDINE. NO MATTER HOW GOOD A PERSON YOU ARE THERE WILL ALWAYS BE SOMEONE CRITICIZING YOU...BY M.C. SKIBUDEE. I AM THANKFUL FOR THE NIGHTS THAT TURNED INTO MORNING, FRIENDS THAT TURNED INTO FAMILY AND DREAMS THAT TURNED INTO REALITY...BY CODEBLACK LIFE. TO BE HAPPY IS TO APPRECIATE THE VALUE OF THIS DAY, OF THIS MOMENT AND OF THOSE WE LOVE WHO ARE WITH US RIGHT HERE AND RIGHT NOW...BY HAPPINESS IN YOUR LIFE. DO WHAT YOU MUST AND YOUR FRIENDS WILL ADJUST...BY

ROBERT BRAULT. BEING HONEST MIGHT NOT GET YOU LOTS OF FRIENDS, BUT IT WILL ALWAYS GET YOU THE RIGHT ONES...SILENCE IS BETTER THAN BULLSHIT...THE PROGRESSIVE RADIO NETWORK.

DESPITE WHAT YOU MAY BELIEVE, YOU CAN DISAPPOINT PEOPLE AND STILL BE GOOD ENOUGH. YOU CAN MAKE MISTAKES AND STILL BE CAPABLE AND TALENTED. YOU CAN LET PEOPLE DOWN AND STILL BE WORTHWHILE AND DESERVING OF LOVE. EVERYONE HAS DISAPPOINTED SOMEONE THEY CARE ABOUT. EVERYONE MESSES UP, LETS PEOPLE DOWN AND MAKES MISTAKES. NOT BECAUSE WE'RE IMPERFECT AND FUNDAMENTALLY HUMAN. EXPECTING ANYTHING DIFFERENT IS SETTING YOURSELF UP FOR FAILURE...BY DANIELL KOEPKE.

BEING TRUE TO YOURSELF MEANS LIVING IN TRUTH WITH EACH PERSON IN YOUR LIFE. IT MEANS REFUSING TO SAY OR DO SOMETHING THAT YOU DON'T BELIEVE IS RIGHT. LIVING IN TRUTH WITH OTHER PEOPLE MEANS THAT YOU REFUSE TO STAY IN ANY SITUATION WHERE YOU ARE UNHAPPY WITH THE BEHAVIOUR OF ANOTHER PERSON. YOU REFUSE TO TOLERATE IT. YOU REFUSE TO COMPROMISE...BY BRAIN TRACY.

DON'T WORRY ABOUT WHAT OTHERS THINK, JUST FOCUS ON YOURSELF AND STAY POSITIVE. SOME PEOPLE ARE ALWAYS NEGATIVE, SO DON'T LET IT BOTHER YOU...BY LESSONS LEARNED IN LIFE.

STOP HOLDING ONTO PEOPLE WHO KEEP LETTING GO OF YOU. PAY ATTENTION TO THE FAITHFUL PEOPLE. THE ONES YOU DON'T HAVE TO IMPRESS. THE ONES WHO ALWAYS HAVE YOUR BACK...THE ONES THAT LOVE YOU WITH NO STRINGS ATTACHED...AS YOU MOVE FORWARD IN LIFE, YOU MAY NEED TO CHANGE YOUR CIRCLES OF FRIENDS. EVERYONE AROUND YOU ISN'T INTERESTED IN SEEING YOU IMPROVE...BY TRINA.

SUCCESSFUL PEOPLE BUILD EACH OTHER UP. THEY MOTIVATE, INSPIRE AND PUSH EACH OTHER. UNSUCCESSFUL PEOPLE JUST HATE, BLAME AND COMPLAIN...BY VICKI YOHE. ONCE YOU CHARACTERISE A MAN BY HIS ACTIONS, YOU WILL NEVER BE FOOLED BY HIS WORDS...BY DR FARRAH GRAY.

YOU CAN GIVE A PERSON KNOWLEDGE, BUT YOU CAN'T MAKE THEM THINK. SOME PEOPLE WANT TO REMAIN FOOLS, ONLY BECAUSE THE TRUTH REQUIRES CHANGE...BY TONY GASKINS. TEN PAINFUL TRUTHS 1)THE AVERAGE HUMAN LIFE IS RELATIVELY SHORT. 2)YOU ONLY EVER LIVE THE LIFE YOU CREATE FOR YOURSELF. 3)BEING BUSY DOES NOT MEAN BEING PRODUCTIVE. 4)SOME KINDER FAILURE OCCURS BEFORE SUCCESS. 5)THINKING AND DOING ARE TWO VERY DIFFERENT THINGS. 6)YOU DON'T HAVE TO WAIT FOR AN APOLOGY TO FORGIVE. 7)SOME PEOPLE ARE SIMPLY, THE WRONG MATCH FOR YOU. 8)IT'S NOT OTHER PEOPLE'S JOB TO LOVE YOU; IT'S YOURS. 9)WHAT YOU OWN IS NOT WHO YOU ARE. 10)EVERYTHING CHANGES, EVERY SECOND...BY SUE FITZMAURICE.

STRONG PEOPLE STAND UP FOR THEMSELVES, BUT THE STRONGEST PEOPLE STAND UP FOR OTHERS...BE SOMEONE'S HERO...BY GEORGE TAKEI. ONE OF THE WORST MISTAKES YOU CAN MAKE IS TO WALK AWAY FROM THE PERSON WHO STOOD THERE AND WAITING FOR YOU. NEVER LEAVE LOYALTY...BY TRENT SHELTON.

MY ATTITUDE IS A RESULT OF YOUR ACTIONS! SO IF YOU DON'T LIKE MY ATTITUDE BLAME YOURSELF...BY BAISDEN LIVE. I BELIEVE IN SECOND CHANCES, I JUST DON'T THINK EVERYONE DESERVES THEM...BY BASIDEN LIVE.

NEVER BE AFRAID TO RAISE YOUR VOICE FOR HONESTY AND TRUTH AND COMPASSION, AGAINST INJUSTICE AND LYING AND GREED. IF PEOPLE ALL OVER THE WORLD DID THIS, IT WOULD CHANGE THE EARTH...BY WILLIAM FAULKNER. THE WORST DISTANCE BETWEEN TWO PEOPLE IS MISUNDERSTANDING.

I DON'T TRUST PEOPLE WHO DON'T LOVE THEMSELVES AND YET TELL ME, "I LOVE YOU". THERE IS AN AFRICAN SAYING WHICH IS; BE CAREFUL WHEN A NAKED MAN OFFERS YOU A SHIRT...BY MAYA ANGELEOU.

# Chapter 4: GOD; YOU & The world.

DEAR GOD, ENLIGHTEN WHAT'S DARK IN ME? STRENGTHEN WHAT'S WEAK IN ME?...MEND WHAT'S BROKEN IN ME? BIND WHAT'S BRUISED IN ME? HEAL WHAT'S SICK IN ME? AND LASTLY REVIVE WHATEVER PEACE AND LOVE THAT HAS DIED IN ME?"...BY VINCENT HAPPY MNISI.

God gave humankind a soul, which is righteousness in nature proving that God lives in all humans. The nature of man is human nature and the nature of God is righteousness. God's love can't be explained, only experienced. You are a child of God and a heir of eternity. God knows you, and you belong to him...By Martyn Lloyd-Jones. We may have different religions, different languages, different coloured skin. But we belong to one human race...By #RehabiTime. When God has selected you, it doesn't matter who else has rejected or neglected you. God's favour outweighs all opposition, you are a winner!...By Spiritualinspiration. Put a smile on your face because God is turning things in your favour...By Hertyborngreatmusic.

Sometimes God calms the storm, sometimes he lets the storm rage and calm his child. When you let God into your life, the storms of life may rise but you will not be shaken...By Pastor Matthew Hagee. "Only God can give you the love you are looking for, and only God can give you the person that loves him enough to deserve you...Rehabtime. Pray is a way to talk to God, I bet you if you pray to God to protect you from your enemies, that you will start losing people you thought were your friends...Vincent Happy Mnisi. Give thanks to the lord for he is good; his love endures forever...Psalm 107:1

God is preparing you for new things, but you have got to let go of some old friends and habits. It may be difficult, but it will be worth it! When you believe in your purpose, you can work through obstacles, overcome disappointments, and endure hardship...by Billy Cox. Fear imprisons, Faith liberates; Fear paralyzes, Faith empowers; Fear disheartens, Faith encourages; Fear sickens, Faith heals; Fear makes useless, Faith makes serviceable...By Harry Emerson Fosdick. Pray not to because you need something but because you have a lot to be thankful for. Advise your sons and daughters, above all else to get to know God and seek his will for their lives. If they make that their priority, they will find him...By Dr James Dobbson.

Faith is seeing light with your heart when all your eyes sees is darkness. God will sometimes end a relationship for your protection...So stop chasing after the person he is trying to save you from...By Trent Shelton. May there be peace in the world and may it begin with me...By Anna Taylor. The omniscience of God is the principle that God is all knowing; that he encompasses all knowledge of the universe past, present and future. In the beginning God created the world and everything in it including knowledge...By Kenni Gambo. "Without dreams, we reach nothing. Without love, we feel nothing. And without God, we are nothing...By DJ Euphonik.

Be strong and courage's, do not be afraid or terrified because of them, for the lord your god goes with you; he will never leave you nor forsake you...Deuteronomy 31 v 6. Ephesians 3:20 I declare over my life, God will do exceedingly, abundantly above all that I ask or think. Because I honour him, his blessings will chase me down and overtake me. I will be in the right place at the right time. People will go out of their way to be good to me, I am surrounded by God's favour...This is my declaration. No matter where you've been, no matter what you've done, realise today that your destiny supersedes your mistakes. When God designed the plan for your life, it wasn't dependent on you being perfect, never making mistakes or never taking a wrong turn. No God knew we would all make mistakes, he knows how to get you back on track no matter where you are in life. Just like there are many routes on a map, God has a plan to help you reach your destination. He has detours, shortcuts and bypasses, He has already calculated the entire route for your life. Today, if you're feeling you've blown it, if you feel like you are too old, too far gone or too far of track know that nothing you've done, no mistakes that you have made will surprise God. He has already got it, figured out. He has arranged a comeback for your setbacks, He has graced your weakness. He has mercy for every failure, his gifts are irrevocable. So rise up in faith and receive the good things he has in store for you!...By Joel Osteen Ministries.

Everyone has an inheritance in Christ. Hebrew 9v16 is communications in faith accepting and proclaiming your problems by faith, the new creation has eternal life, meaning that you have the same life as Jesus Christ and have become as righteous in the nature as God does...God live in us, in everybody you can find God's nature living in them, our souls houses the living God, we as humans must be glad that our reflection in the mirror is like looking at the image of God as he made each one of us in his own image, I must add that I have personally seen a supernatural being while under-arrest in Grahams-Town, his body was made of light, his complexion was like a radiant light and he had long white hair and a beard...By Vincent Happy Mnisi.

As you grow closer to God, your circle of friends will get smaller...By Dr Farrah Gray. God wants what is best for you, Don't settle for anything less...By Positivity Inspires. The enemy always fights the hardest when he knows God has something Great in store for you...By GodsNotDead. Be patient. Don't lose faith. Prayers come true unexpectedly. Trust in Gods timing. It's perfect...By #RehabTime.

Faith is believing and telling yourself that no matter what lies ahead, God is already there. You cannot control what happens to you, but you can control your attitude towards what happens to you, and in that, you will be mastering change rather than allowing it to master you. By Brian Tracey. Are we not all children of God? In truth, not one of us can ever stop being a child of God. By Russell M. Nelson. For I am not ashamed of the Gospel, because it is the power of God that brings salvation to everyone who believes...Romans 1 v 16. The more the world tries to discourage you, the more God will encourage you"...By Pastor Matthew Hagee.

The devil is always seeking to lead us away from ourselves, from what God is calling us to, be alert for distractions and pointless living. Believe in yourself, for you are a child of God. If we have tasted the true wealth of the Kingdom and beheld the true riches of God, having a lot of money, or a little, will not be of concern to us...By Rick Joyner.

"I pray that, you all put your shoes way under the bed at night so that you gotta get on your knees in the morning to find them! And while you're down there thank God for his grace and mercy and understanding"...By Denzel Washington.

"God grant me the serenity to accept the things I cannot change, courage to change the things I can, and the wisdom to know the difference...Unknown. When you ask God to show you the truth about someone, be certain you are ready for the revelation because reality is not always pretty...By Positivity Inspires.

"Inequality is the root to social evil"...By Pope Francis. God will give you a job making more money then you've ever imagined with a position you're not even educationally qualified for, it's called favour. The devil had a plot but God has a plan. Blowing out someone's candle doesn't make yours shine any brighter...By Mind Unleashed. "God is working things out for you, even when you don't feel it. Have faith and be thankful"...By Vincent Happy Mnisi. God will wreck your plans when he sees that your plans are about to wreck you, and sometimes you have to look up and smile and say "I know that was you God! and Thanks!.. Realise how blessed you are...By Vincent Happy Mnisi. "God will make a way for you were there seems to be no way, if you have faith he can move mountains and part the sea for your safe passage. If you fight all your battles on your knees, you will win all the time"... by Charles .F. Stanley.  The greatest test of faith is when you don't get what you want, but still you are able to say thank you Lord...by Pastor Mathew Hagee.

"Where you are today is no accident, God is using the situation you are in right now to shape you and prepare you for the place he wants to bring you into tomorrow. Trust him with his plan even if you don't understand it"...by Empowered Woman of faith and purpose Inc. Make the choice to do what is right. Some people may not like it. Others may walk out of your life, because of it but God will be pleased with your decision...by Positivity Inspires. "Even during your darkest moments, God still has a plan for you to shine bright. Don't lose faith"...by Rahabitime.

Isn't it amazing how God brings the right people into your life at the right time, people who support, love and pray for you, regardless of your circumstances...By Vincent Happy Mnisi. "You must be obedient to God's will before the Holy Spirit can work in you. Better to be poor and honest than a rich person no one can trust. Ignorant zeal is worthless; haste makes waste. People ruin their lives by their own stupidity, so why does God always get blamed? Wealth attracts friends as honey draws flies, but poor people are avoided like a plague. Lots of people flock around a generous person; everyone's is a friend to the philanthropist, but when you are down on your luck, even your family avoids you, yes even your best friends wish you would get lost. If they see you coming, they look the other way...out of sight, out of mind. Grow a wise heart...You will do yourself a favour, keep a clear head, you will find a good life. The person who tells lies gets caught; the person who spreads rumours is ruined...by Book of Proverbs.

God says "The reason some people have turned against you and walked away from you without reason, has nothing to do with you. It is because I have removed them from your life because they cannot go where I am taking you next. They will only hinder you in your next level because they have already served their purpose in your life. Let them go and keep moving. Greater is coming." Say's the Lord. Galatians 5: 16-26 Walk in the Spirit: "I say then walk in the Spirit, and you shall not fulfil the lust of the flesh. For the flesh lusts against the spirit, and the spirit against the flesh, and these are contrary to one another, so that you do not do the things that you wish. But if you are led by the spirit, you are not under the law. Now the works of the flesh are evident which are 1)Adultery 2)Fornication 3)Uncleanness 4)Lewdness 5)Idolatry 6)Sorcery 7)Hatred 8)Contentions 9)Jealousies 10)Outburst of wrath 11)Selfish ambitions 12)Dissensions 13)Heresies 14)Envy 15)Murder 16)Drunkenness 17)Revelries and the likes of which I tell you beforehand, just as I told you in time past, that those who practice such things will not inherit the Kingdom of God. But the fruit of the spirit is love, joy, peace, long suffering, kindness, goodness, faithfulness, gentleness and self-control. Against such there is no law. And those who are with Christ have crucified the flesh with its passions and desires. If we live in the spirit, let us also walk in the spirit let us not become conceited, provoking one another, envying one another...By Jesus Christ.

"Keep talking about me behind my back, and watch God keep blessing me in front of your face!...by Vincent Happy Mnisi. What is coming will make sense of what is happening. Let God finish his work...By A woman of faith. "When money is your God, you will lose your moral, dignity, self-respect, integrity, friends and people you love in the process of obtaining it...Unknown. "I made the universe out of nothing, trust me, I can take care of you"...By God. I told God "protect me from my enemies and I started losing people I thought were friends...Basiden Live. Those who put their trust in God will never be disappointed. Your best is yet to come, stop letting people who do little for you, control so much of your time, life and emotions...By Vincent Happy Mnisi.

Don't allow people to redirect you. Many will try to steer you away from your God-given purpose, but you must stay on course...By Positivity Inspires. "I can't wait until this storm is over so I can tell you "How God Challenged me, how I made it through and how I am a better person because of it"...By Odell Beckham Jr. God didn't redeem you so that you could produce sour grapes of doubt, gossip and criticism...By Pastor Matthew Hagee. Thank you, Lord for the times you came through for us when we didn't even know we needed rescuing...By Crosswalk.com.

God has a reason for allowing things to happen. We may never understand his wisdom, but we simply have to trust his will. The light of God surrounds me, the love of God enfolds me. The power of God protects me, the presence of God watches over me. Wherever I am, God is there always...By Vincent Happy Mnisi. I declare all that I have is yours God. And all that I want comes from or through you. I place my ego, my desire, my dreams at your feet...by Mark Brown.

Not once does the Bible say "Worry about it"; "Stress over it" or "Figure it out" but over and over it clearly says, "Trust God." As Christians we sometimes have the tendency to blame everything on the Devil...but sometimes it's simply the consequences of the choices that we've made...and God imploring us to be accountable and make a different decision next time...By Meagan Good.

If you stay humble, honest and hungry, there is nothing God cannot do through you!...By Bishop Dale Bronner. You can't fight the whole world, and you can't fight everybody in your world. It's not about giving in, it about letting go...By Sue Fitzmaurice. God sees in you a masterpiece waiting to happen...By GodsNotDead. Just like the stone that rolled away at Jesus's grave, the thing that keeps you from having a breakthrough...God can roll it back and remove it in an instant!...By Pastor John Hagee. Be kind for everyone you meet is fighting a battle you know nothing about...By Maria Shriver. In many instances, when God is about to make a major move in your life, the enemy will strike hard! It's a Must that you cling to the Lord. When you do this, then the devils attack can't stop you...By Positivity Inspires.

Once you receive God's approval to make that move, don't keep putting it off. Procrastination delays progress...By Positivity Inspires. "The most serious of the evils that afflict the world these days are youth unemployment and the loneliness of the old. The old need care and companionship; the young need work and hope but have neither one nor the other and the problem is they don't even look for them anymore"...By Pope Francis. If you stay humble, honest and hungry, there is nothing God cannot do through you!...By Bishop Dale. C Bronner. The Angel of death can greet you anytime and anywhere...By Pompey Diddley Doo. You can't fight the whole world and you can't keep fighting everyone in your world. It's not about giving in; it's about letting go...By Sue Fitzmaurice

Good sees in you a masterpiece waiting to happen...By GodsNotDead. God is preparing you for new things, but you've got to let go of some old friends and habits. It may be difficult, but it's worth it...By Bishop Dale C. Bronner. God has your best interest at heart. When a door closes, you don't know what God is saving you from...By Joel Osteen. Don't let the abundance of God's gifts cause you to forget him...By Godfruits.com. What God knows about me is more important than what others think about me...By GodsNotDead. The purpose of life is to glorify God in both good and hard times alike...By T.B. Joshua.

This is my command...be strong and courageous! Do not be afraid or discouraged. For the Lord your God is with you wherever you go"...Joshua 1V9 NLT. Did you know that fear works just like faith but in the opposite direction? Faith opens the door for God to work in our lives; fear opens the door for the enemy to work in our lives...Unknown.

Anything arranged and operated by the Lord will succeed. So let God lead it, and watch it flourish in due season ...By Positivity Inspires \god doesn't simply renovate the past. He makes all things new...By Faith.com. Love the Lord your God with all your heart and with all your soul and with all your mind and with all your strength...Mark 12V30. If you only pray when you're in trouble...you're in trouble... By One Spark Foundation. When we understand our relationship to God, we also understand our relationship to one another. All men and women on this earth are the offspring of God. Spirit brothers and sisters...By Dallin H. Oaks.

Stop waiting on other people to give you permission to do what God already appointed you to do!...By Shanel Cooper-Sykes. If you are going through hell keep going...By Lynda Fields Life Coach. How can God remove your pain if you're not removing yourself from the situation...By Joel Osteen. And Give thanks for everything to God; There lives we live, the food we eat, and for our loved ones, Lord, help us all to live our days with thankful hearts and loving ways...By Every bad situation will have something positive. Even a dead clock show correct time twice a day. Stay positive in life. God know what is best for us...By. Instead of falling apart and thinking! I can't believe this is happening" Your attitude should be "It's just another weed, no big  deal. I didn't sow it. I don't have to reap it. God said he would take care of it...By Joel Osteen.

God always leads us to where we need to be not where we want to be"...By The Lord is my shepherd, I shall not want. Christ is beside me, before me, behind me, within me and above me...By familyshare.com. God, please strengthen those who are tired of holding on and those that feel forgotten, Send them a sign that you are there, and restore hope. In Jesus name, Amen!...By Manny Garcia.

"For I know the plans I have for you" declared the LORD, "Plans to prosper you and not to harm you, plans to give you hope and future"...Jeremiah 29 v 11. Expect the best, expect the favour of God on your life...By Dandi Krakowski. What God lifts up, no person can push down...By Life Is Possible. If you have time to pray, God had time to listen...By Life Is Possible. You don't have any problem that the Lord can't solve...By Life Is Possible.

When people underestimate you, God sees potential...We can't do things on our won, but we can do all things through Christ Jesus. Give it some time, your naysayers will see the Lord work through you and God will get all the glory...By Positivity Inspires. Prayer is the most important conversation of the day. Take it to God, before you take it to anyone else...By GodsNotDead. The peace of God transcends all understanding...Philippines 4 v 7. Sometimes God works secretly and behind the scenes. But he will reveal his work to us when the time is right...By GodsNotDead. God is faithful yesterday, today and always...By Pureflix. Just because you have found God, doesn't mean you should cease seeking him even more...By Vincent Happy Mnisi.

God is working all things together for your good. He has a master plan for your life...By Joel Osteen. There are people God has placed in your life who are waiting for you to speak God's word over them. It doesn't help them if you just feel for them and keep it inside...By Joel Osteen. Thank you Lord for protecting me from what I thought I wanted and placing in my life what I knew I needed...By #RehabTime. Sometimes God will bring a person in your life not to stay, but to introduce you to someone who will. Every season has its purpose...By RehabTime.

God has a purpose for your life before you ever had a plan for yourself. Sometimes your plans have to fail, so God's purpose for your life can prevail. He knows what's best for you...By RehabTime. Everything you're going through is just preparing you for everything that God has called you to be...Don't let the struggle take your faith, let it strengthen it...By Trent Shelton.

You are alive alright? You have God's approval to live your life...By Vincent Happy Mnisi.


Stop trying to get noticed by people you're already approved by God...By Trent Shelton. God is about to take you where you could not go on your own. God doesn't care how smart you are. He cares about what's in your heart...By Monica (Touched By An Angel). God has a plan and purpose for you; He will not fail you!...By Pastor John Hagee. When God is with you, Goodness and Mercy chase you down and you shall prosper!...By Pastor Matthew Hagee. Alive; Blessed; Grateful; God is Good!!!...By Iman. You cannot make it in this world without God...By Lamarr Houston.

To those I may have wronged, I ask forgiveness. To those I may have helped, I wish I did more. To those I neglected to help, I ask for understanding. To those who helped me, I sincerely thank you so much...By Shashicka Tyre-Hill.If you have a well-used bible that is falling apart, then you will have a life that's not...By Adrian Rogers. Everything the enemy has stolen, God is going to restore: The Joy, the peace, the health, the dreams...By Shashicka Tyre-Hill. For the Kingdom of God does not consist in words but in Power...1 Corinthians 4 V20...By GodsNotDead. It is God's will that you be used for your highest purpose, the key to unlocking your best future begins with an understanding of purpose...By T. D. Jakes. If God called you, he won't change his mind...By T. D. Jakes.

Satan cannot take from you and you cannot lose that which the blood of Jesus cannot restore...By Rob Parsley. I belong to Jesus who paid a great price for me...By Bible book. Nothing happens for nothing, "As Christians your troubles become easier to handle when you know that it will not last long"...By T.B. Joshua Ministries. Let us hear the conclusion of the whole matter: Fear God, and keep his commandments: For this is the duty of man...Ecclesiastes 12V 13

KJV. Most things we set out to accomplish in life take an extensive process. In all honesty, walking with God in pure holiness and commitment, and strengthening your fate are life-long pursuits...By T. D. Jakes.

It is a great thing to be a child of God, and joint heir with Jesus Christ. If this is your privilege. You will know the fellowship of Christ suffering...By Ellen G. White. Heavenly father, keep a keen watch over me as I dress for another day of battle. Temptation and evil will try to overcome me and sway me from you, but dressed in your armour, I know that I will successfully defend against each

attack...Amen. Would you please talk to me? I want to tell you how much I love you...By God. Your positive thoughts are both the prayer and the answer to your prayers...By Bryant McGill. Even in your darkest moments God will see you through...By Herty Borngreat.music.

If you ask anything in my name, I will do it...John 14 v14. Be more concerned with what God thinks about you, than what people think about you...By Doris Nelson. When God bless you, he really blesses you. However the Lord doesn't give us things with the intentions of it taking our attention away from him. Use whatever God had given you for his glory and as you continually advance in life, don't forget your beginning...Remember that it was the Lord who brought you to that point, and it is he who will take you even further in life...By Positivity Inspires. You are never to lost to be saved...By Vicki Yohe. Is prayer your steering wheel or your spare tire...By God's Not Dead.

The storm of life might knock me down, but God will pick me up. I have a mighty saviour who loves me and cares for me...Thank you Jesus. Nothing lasts forever, not even your problems. Stop worrying and get on with the awesome life God's given you...By GodVine.com. The Lord is my light and my salvation, whom shall I fear? The Lord is the strength of my life; of whom shall I be afraid?...Psalm 27 V 1.

You can't walk with God holding hands with the devil...By Shashicka Tyre-Hill. You can't trust everyone you break bread with Ask Jesus...By Earnest Pugh. Life isn't about finding yourself. It's about discovering who God created you to be...By Gods Not Dead. Make the choice to do what is right. Some people may not like it. Others may walk out of your life. If it feels right to you let them walk out...By Vincent Happy  Mnisi. God isn't an option, He is a necessity!...By Christianet.com. If you have God you have everything that you need...By Victoria Osteen. God never promised the absence of storms in our life. But he does  promise  to walk with us through them...By Crosswalk.com. I raised you up to demonstrate my power in you, and that my name might be proclaimed throughout the whole earth...Romans 9 Verse 17. God did not turn his back on me. He was carrying me instead...By  Tracie Miles. Grace means that all your mistakes now serve a purpose instead of serving shame...By Faith.com.


Instead of complaining about what's wrong, thank God for what's right...By Joel Osteen. Therefore I say to you, whatever things you ask when you pray, believe you receive them, and you will have them...Mark 11 Verse 24.

When you pray be sure that you also listen. You have things you want to say to God. But he also has things he wants to say to you...By Good fruits.com. I am Grateful, Father, that you love me and that your LOVE is perfect and Unconditional. Help me to learn to receive your love by faith and go through each day knowing that I am valuable because I am loved by my heavenly Father...By Joyce Meyer.

When have the believe that God is in control. That means there is no need to be stressed out or worried...By Joel Osteen. Peace is seeing the sunset and knowing who to thank...By Alessandra Ambrosio. Thank you for the many blessings that came my way today...By Incredible Joy. I will not be defined by my sin as I am refined by the cross...By Mark Brown. God remembers my sins no more...Hebrew 8 V 12. Man can't stop what God is doing. Get ready for your blessings. They are on the way!...By Tony Gaskins. Be thankful for unknown blessings already on their way...By Motivation For Women. An abundance of blessings are being created for me now, I'm ready to receive them with joy and love...By Emmanuel Dagher.

God speaks to those who take time to listen and he listens to those who take time to pray...By Bible God Quotes.com. I am a child of God, Highly favoured blessed overcomer...By I am a Child of God. The blessing of the Lord, it maketh and he addeth so sorrow with it...Proverbs 10:22 KJV. Father, when I am faced with a difficult situation, help me to choose joy in spite of my circumstance. I thank you that your joy is my strength each and everyday...By Joyce Meyer. Let your fears go, lest they make you faint-hearted. Stop inspiring fear in those around you and now take your stand in faith. God has been good; He will continue to manifest his goodness. Let us approach these days expecting to see the goodness of the Lord manifest. Let us, be strong and of good courage; The Lord will fight for us, if we stand in faith...By Francis Frangipane.

You cannot receive any other gifts from God until you receive the gift of salvation...By Pastor Matthew Hagee. Dear God Thank you for being there when nobody else was. God has a bigger plan for me...Faith creates a space in your life that lets the miracles in...By Sarah Rajkotwala. Sometimes God prunes our branches for us, even removing items that we may enjoy that aren't strengthening our faith...By FaithWords. God sometimes takes us into troubled waters, not to drown us but to cleanse us...By Shashicka Tyre-Hill. God doesn't make average moves, When God moves in your life it will make people scratch their heads in wonder. Get ready for a mighty move...By Tony Gaskins. I love you Lord! Thank you for loving me!...By Trust in the Lord. God, I pray that I will represent you well today. That I will Glorify you in all I do Amen...By Pure Flix. Hard times, Bad times or Tough times. I still have faith in God...By familyshare.com. Faith=Trust without reservation!...By Vincent Happy Mnisi.

When I am in line with my dream and goals in life, even though I pass through the valley of the shadow of death, I fear no one because the lord is with me...By T. B. Joshua. Continue to work out your salvation without fear and trembling, for it is God who works in you to will and to act in order to fulfil his good purpose...Philippines 2: 12to13 The bible people.com. As men we need accountability and responsibility. We need to stop seeking praise for every good deed and start seeking correction for our shortcomings. We need to become what the world needs man. Stop making excuses. Stop bailing out. Stop taking shortcuts. When God gave us dominion he didn't say it would be easy. It's time to man up!...By Tony Gaskins.

My help comes from the Lord God, who made Haven and Earth...By Vincent Happy Mnisi. Trust this when God says it's your time, no one can stop it!...By Shashicka Tyre-Hill. All things work together for good to those who love God...Romans 8:28. All the Christmas presents in the world are worth nothing without the presence of Christ...By Kirk Camerons. Storms and struggles may come, but I belong to God, who makes all things new and protects me from evil. Thank you Lord!...By lovecoverallmovie.com

Some days are easier than others, if you're having a challenging time, let your Angles wrap you in their wings and remind you how loved you are...By Anna Taylor. Don't repay evil with evil. Don't retaliate with insults when people insult you. Instead pay them back with a blessing. That is what God has called you to do and he will grant with blessings...By Vincent Happy Mnisi.

Perfection is a man-made concept that people can't even agree on, let alone actually actually reach. Instead God just wants you do your best with the gifts you've been given. Help some people, be generous. Keep striving to be your best at your own standards. You will one day soon get your reward...By Vincent Happy Mnisi. My flesh and my heart may fail, but God is the strength of my heart and my portion forever...Psalm 73:26. Those who leave everything in God's hands will eventually see God's hands in every-thing...By TBN Trinity Broadcasting Network. He who kneels before GOD can stand before anyone...By Fameus Redds.

Your worth isn't based on your social status, relationship status, or work status but on your heavenly status. You are God's Child...By daugtherbydesign. For I am not ashamed of the Gospel, because it is the Power of God that brings salvation to everyone who believes...Romans 1:16. God has placed you where you're at in this very moment for a reason, remember that and trust he is working everything out!...By kenny Lattimore.

Guide me through this darkness, Lord. Especially when I cannot seem to hold on for another moment. Flood me with the graces of hope and fortitude. Send your angles to watch over me as I sleep through the night. Remind me during the day that from this small dark cocoon. I will emerge a butterfly...By Caroline Myss.

Your greatest test is when you, are able to bless someone else while you are going through your own storm...By Shashicka Tyre-Hill. Jesus sees the end from the beginning...Robert Murray McCheyne. If God allowed me to lose it then he's going to replace it with something's which are much better...By Praise 104.1 FM radio.

God works the night-shift, not you. Don't spend another sleepless night trying to figure out your issues, trust that the LORD is working it out...By Farrah Gray. It's never too late to start over, chase your dreams, create healthy relationships, understand Gods power, change your ways, be positive, have hope, accept the Lord, make a difference, forgive the people that hurt you, learn something new, Do what you have always wanted to do, Say I am sorry, get inspired, begin again and put your past in your past...By Vincent Happy Mnisi.

You are and I am a child of of God...By Vincent Happy Mnisi. Dear God if today I lose my hope, please remind me that your plans are better than my dreams...By Vincent Happy Mnisi. I can do all things through Christ who strengths me. God will make a way when there seems to be no way...By My bible.com. Mortals make elaborate plans, but GOD has the last word. Humans are satisfied with whatever looks good; GOD probes for what is good. Put GOD in charge of your work, then what you've planned will take place. GOD made everything with a place and purpose; even the wicked are included—but for judgement. GOD can't stomach arrogance or pretence; believe me, he'll put those upstarts in their place. Guilt is banished through love and truth; Fear-of-GOD deflects evil. When GOD approves of your life, even your enemies will end up shaking your hand. Far better to be right and poor than to be wrong and rich. We plan the way we want to live, but only GOD makes us able to live it. A good leader motivates, doesn't mislead, doesn't exploit. GOD cares about honesty in the workplace; your business is his business. Good leaders abhor wrongdoing of all kinds; sound leadership has a moral foundation. Good leaders cultivate honest speech; they love advisor's who tell them the truth. An intemperate leader wreaks havoc in lives; you're smart to stay clear of someone like that. Good-tempered leaders invigorate lives; they're like spring rain and sunshine. Get wisdom—it's worth more than money; choose insight over income every time. The road of right living bypasses evil; watch your step and save your life. First pride, then the crash— the bigger the ego, the harder the fall. It's better to live humbly among the poor than to live it up among the rich and famous. It pays to take life seriously; things work out when you trust in GOD.

A wise person gets known for insight; gracious words add to one's reputation. True intelligence is a spring of fresh water, while fools sweat it out the hard way. They make a lot of sense, these wise folks; whenever they speak, their reputation increases. Gracious speech is like clover honey— good taste to the soul, quick energy for the body. There's a way that looks harmless enough; look again—it leads straight to hell. Appetite is an incentive to work; hunger makes you work all the harder. Mean people spread mean gossip; their words smart and burn. Troublemakers start fights; gossips break up friendships. Calloused climbers betray their very own friends; they'd stab their own grandmothers in the back. A shifty eye betrays an evil intention; a clenched jaw signals trouble ahead. Gray hair is a mark of distinction, the award for a God-loyal life. Moderation is better than muscle, self-control better than political power. Make your motions and cast your votes, but GOD has the final say. (Proverbs 16:1-33 MSG)

I have told you these things, so that in me you may have peace. In this world you will have trouble. But take heart! I have overcome the world...By Jesus Christ John 16:33. God's to TEN 1) Put God first. 2) Worship him only 3) No Bad words 4) Work & rest 5) Obey your parents 6) Harm no one 7) Don't cheat 8) Tell the truth 9) Listen 10) Don't be jealous of other people's stuff.

Sometimes God uses pain to inspect us, correct us, direct us and perfect us...By Wisdomfeed. At this exact very moment, the angles are sprinkling extra-glittery goodness on your path. Take a breath you are doing fine. Your job is to show up and be you. Let the universe take care of the rest. Enjoy the ride, Cool things are happening. Savor the sweetness of the moment. It's just the beginning of a new amazing adventures. Remember Gods dream of you is much bigger than our own. Shine on. Your life is blessed...By Illuminating Sounds.

If nobody got me, I know God got me, can I get an Amen!...By Dr Farrah Gray. Wait on the Lord. Don't rush into something that is not approved by Him. What God has reserved for you for is better. Remain patient...By Positivity Inspires.

Even in your darkest moment God will see you through...By Herty BornGreatMusic. The Lord will not send you unprepared or unequipped. Work with what God gives you. It is enough to accomplish the task...By Positivity Inspires.


Heavenly father when I am tired, you give me the strength to go on. When discouraged you give me hope. When I am afraid, You are my peace...Amen...I love Jesus Christ...No power of hell, no scheme of Man! Could ever pluck me from God's Hands!.. By Vincent Happy Mnisi.

I heard the Lord say, I didn't come to send you BACKWARDS, I came to LIFT you UP and move you FOWARD!...by Dale. C. Bronner. I will be with you always, even until the end of the world...By Jesus Christ Matthew 28:20. Give thanks to the Lord for he is good, his love endures forever...Psalm 118:29. The Lord will fight for you; you need only be still...Exodus 14:14. Nothing you have is because of luck or chance. It's all due to God's grace and favour...By Shashicka Tyre-Hill.

God knows how to get you back on track no matter where you are in life...By Kenny Lattimore. Dear God no matter what happens give me the heart that is willing to obey you whatever the cost maybe...Love me...By The Bible Book. Trust me: When God says its your time, no one can stop it!!! By Vincent Happy Mnisi.

When a train goes through a tunnel and it gets dark, you don't throw away the ticket and jump off. You sit still and trust the engineer, Trust God today no matter how dark your situation, God says "You are coming out"...By the Church at New Bern. If God shuts a door, stop banging on it. Trust whatever is behind it is not meant for you...By Shashicka Tyre-Hill. God isn't an option, he's necessity!...By Christian.net.com

Learn to rest, restore, rebuild, renew, refresh. Take a sabbatical from the stress and demands of life. Learn to focus on what God has done for you instead of what you want you are waiting on him to do!...By Bishop C. Bronner.

Sometimes God pours out His power in ways you don't expect or through people whom you don't particularly like. When He does, will you stand by or will you receive His anointing...By Pastor Ken Gott.

# Chapter 5: Love!!!...

Love cannot be found where it doesn't exist there's a difference between being patient with someone and wasting your time...By Vincent Happy Mnisi. A man with dreams needs a woman with vision. Her perspective, faith and support will change his reality, if she does not challenge you then she is not good for you. Men who want to stay ordinary will tell you not to have expectations of them, men who want to be great will expect you to push them, pray with them and invest in them"...Unknown. "Love isn't a transaction but a gift freely given. We should love without expecting anything in return"...By Mark Brown.

"Someone who is worthy of your love will never put you in a situation where you feel you must sacrifice your dignity, your integrity, or yourself worth to be with them"...Unknown. "A woman's loyalty is tested when her man has nothing...A man's loyalty is tested when he has everything"...By Baisden Live. The best thing in life is finding someone who knows all your flaws, mistakes, and weakness and still thinks you're amazing. By Hayon Sop Williams.

Ten ways to love (1)Listen without interrupting(Proverb 18).(2)Speak without accusing(James 1:19). (3)Give without sparing (Proverbs 21v26). (4) Pray without ceasing(Colossians 1v9). (5)Answer without arguing(Proverbs 17v1). (6)Share without pretending(Ephesians 4v15). (7)Enjoy without compliant (Philippines 2v14). (8)Trust without wavering(1 Corinthians 13v7). (9)Forgive without punishing(Colossians 3v13). (10)Promise without forgetting...By Empowered woman of faith and purpose. The preparation of the heart belongs to men, but the answer from the tongue is from the lord (Matthew 12v25). There is no need to rush, if something is meant to be, it will happen in the right time, with the right person and for the right reasons...By Vincent Happy Mnisi.

Patience is not about how long someone can wait, it's about how well they behaved while they wait...by I fight with u, cuz I luv u so much. "Don't pick a woman just because she will look good in the team uniform, choose a woman who won't quit the team if you hit a losing streak!..."You love with your heart, but you first lust with your eyes...By Vincent Happy Mnisi.


We live in a world where we have to hide to make love, while violence is practised in broad daylight...By Baisden Live. When you care for someone more than their deserve, you get hurt more than you deserve. Life is about balance, be kind but don't let people abuse , but don't be deceived. Be content, but never but never stop improving yourself... . I just wanna say...Life is too short to worry about stupid things. Have fun, fall in love, regret nothing and don't let people bring you down. By Marcelo Santos III. Forgive and move on, don't hold on to hate. They hurt you, but you'll hurt even more if you refuse to forgive. Let it go so you can prepare to receive all that you deserve from life. By Tony Gaskins. Keep your heart of compassion open...By Joel Osteen. Returning hate for hate multiplies hate, adding deeper darkness to a night already devoid of stars...By Martin Luther King Jr. You have to speak to be heard, but sometimes you have to be silent to be appreciated. The most hurtful thing you can say to someone is to say nothing...Unknown.

It's crazy how you can go for months or years without talking to someone but they still cross your mind every day. By Vincent Happy Mnisi. Often it is the same story different person, every person you meet claims to want this or that, but what they really desire is things their way. When it truly comes down to it the love of the flesh trumps love in the hearts of many. The common courtesy of love, respect and walking together is tossed out of the window. People rather believe their negative thoughts, fears and opinions of others. Stop claiming, you want love when you have never done anything to really prove you want it. Many are just stuck in the past and repeating the same mistakes, if you want a successful relationship love has to be your badge...By Quentin McCall.

Physical attraction are common, but a mental connection is rare. Once you have the latter, the former will never be enough...by Gregg Braden. "A woman's heart must be so hidden in God, that a man has to seek him to find her"...By Maya Angelou. A real man never stops trying to show a woman how much she means to him, even after he got her. By Love.com.

"Some of the biggest challenges in relationships come from the fact that most people enter a relationship in order to get something; They're trying to find someone who's going to make them feel good. In reality, the only way a relationship will last is if you see your relationship as a place that you go to give, and not a place you go to take...By Anthony Robbins.

10% of conflicts are due to differences in opinion. 90% are due to tone of voice...Wisdom. ,"True love is when you touch someone with your spirit, and in return they touch your soul with their heart...by ."Two things to remember in life. Not all scars show, not all wounds heal. Sometimes you can't see, the pain someone feels...Unknown. The most beautiful people, we have known are those who have known defeat; known suffering; known struggle; known loss and have found their way out of the depths. These people have an appreciation, a sensitivity and an understanding of life that fills them with compassion, gentleness and a deep loving concern, beautiful people do not just happen...unknown. Missing someone isn't about how long it has been since you've seen them or the amount of time since you've talked, it's about that very moment when you find yourself doing something and wishing they were right there by your side...Unknown.

there is a thin line between love and hate, that's for sure. You love a person and then you get to hate them, love is a mystery once you open your heart to someone you are allowing that person to break it which leads to hate. life is for us to live, love is for us to share and loving your life is knowing your purpose in life and pursuing it with all you have...By Vincent Happy Mnisi. If another woman steals your man, there's no better revenge than letting her keep him. Real men can't be stolen...Unknown. A man's biggest mistake is giving another man an opportunity to make his woman smile. Love cannot be found where it doesn't exist there's a difference between being patient with someone and wasting your time. The most hurtful thing you can say to someone is to say nothing at all...by Vincent Happy Mnisi. Women are like the police, they can have all the evidence in the world but they still want a confession...by Baisden Live.

A flower does not think of competing against the flower next to it. It just blooms, so just do your thing and bloom...by Basiden Live. Follow your heart, but don't forget to take your head with you too...by Lyndafields.com. Always tell someone how you feel, because opportunities are lost in the blink of an eye, but regret can last a lifetime...By Killian Bukutu. Forgiveness is the best form of love, it takes a strong person to say they're sorry and even stronger person to forgive. Sometimes being strong and moving on is all you can do...by Lynda Fields Life Coach.

If your relationship has more issues than your magazine, you need to cancel your subscription...by Searchquotes.com. Support those who support you, don't let the people who love you starve because you're trying to feed people who weren't there when you were starving family first...by Tony Gaskin. Be generous, give to those you love; give to those who love you, give to the fortunate, give to the unfortunate, yes, give especially to those you don't want to give. You will receive abundance for your giving. The more you give the more you will have...by Mystic Sounds.

I may not say everything perfectly; I may not do everything perfectly. But if my heart is in the right place, and I try my best, then I am ok with that. No one is perfect...by Anna Pereira. Sometimes life doesn't want to give you something you want, not because you don't deserve it, but because you deserve more...by Killian Bukutu. When it's Right it feels good. When it's Right, there is no battle of the egos. When it's Right you can't wait to be there. When it's Right, the rest of everything that truly Matters falls into place...by Anna Pereira.

Any woman can spend a man's money; ride in his car, and orders off the menu. But only a real woman can help a man achieve his goals in life, support him when he's broke, push him to be successful, shower him with positive energy, compliment him on a regular basis and never kick him while he's down. If you find a woman like that make her your real partner for life. Don't cheat in a relationship, if you are not happy then leave...By Vincent Happy Mnisi. He who finds a wife finds a good thing and obtains favour from the lord..(Proverbs 18v22).

If someone in your life is making you feel worthless: (1) You're not. (2) You're amazing. (3) They don't deserve you. (4) Consider whether you're staying in that relationship...By Sue Fitzmaurice. A pretty face get old...A nice body will change...But a good woman will always be a good woman...by Kathy Wakile. When you live, love and dream with an open heart, all things are possible...by Anna Taylor. When someone loves you, they don't have to say it. You can tell by the way they treat you...By Lil O's. You are worthy of all love and all good simply because you are live!... By Anna Taylor. Everyone comes with baggage, find someone who loves you enough to help you unpack...By Brynne Edelstein.

Just because you're mad at someone doesn't mean you stop loving them...By Verona. Don't be afraid to take a risk your heart leads you to...By Anna Peneira. Five secrets to a perfect relationship: 1) it's important to have a man who helps at home and knows how to cook, clean and has a job. 2) It's important to have a man who can make you laugh. 3) It's important to have a man you can trust and wants only you. 4) It's important to have a man who is good in bed and enjoys being with you. 5) It's absolutely vital that these four men don't know each other...By lifelovesquotesandsayings.com.

Don't go looking for a good woman until you yourself have become a good man. You must meet the requirements of your requirement's...By Baisden Live. Chicks are quick to reject a man who lives with his mother...but will jump into bed with a man who lives with his wife and kids in a heartbeat...By Basiden Live. The worst distance between two people is misunderstanding...By Baisden Live. Today tell a woman she is beautiful, actually do this every day of your life you will soon meet the love of your life and make many female friends...By Vincent Happy Mnisi. If you sit quietly with an open heart, it will find you...By Anna Pereira. I hope love finds you as you search for it where ever it maybe, it could be the girl next door, or a girl on the internet million miles away. Just search with an honest heart you will soon find love...By Vincent Happy Mnisi.

You can't hate yourself happy. You can't criticise yourself thin. You can't shame yourself wealthy. Real change begins with self-love and self-care...By Jessica Ortner.com

A wise physician once said, " The best medicine for humans is love? Someone asked "What if it doesn't work?" He smiled and answered "Increase the dose...Unknown. Be a living, breathing expression of love. There is no need to convince anyone of anything. The most powerful way to teach is by example...By Anna Taylor. A Man has done nothing for you until he has made you a wife. Stop idolising boyfriends...By Vincent Happy Mnisi.

The greatest influence you can have in any situation is to be the presence of love ...By Robert Holden. Never ignore a person who loves you, cares for you, and misses you, because one day, you might wake up and realise you lost the moon while counting the stars...By Zig Ziglar. The highest love a person can have for you is to wish for you to evolve into the best person you can be...By David Viscott.

You cannot heal what you refuse to first acknowledge...By Bryant McGill. So many go into relationships hoping to get something to make them feel complete. When in actuality, a relationship is about sharing who you already are in your wholeness and then bathing in the beauty and adventure of that!....By Shari Alyse.

If you love two people at the same time, choose the second one, because if you really loved the first one you wouldn't have fallen for the second....By

Jonny Depp. Beauty begins the moment you decide to be yourself….By Coco Chanel. One of the cruellest things you can do to another person is pretend to care about them more than you really do….By Doug Coupland. Every man has two men in him, a king and a fool. How do you know you have found your Queen? When she speaks to the King in you…By Farrah Gray.

Ladies…A guy is only insecure about losing his girl when he knows someone else can treat her better…By Farrah Gray. No one can set your level of worthiness except you…By Bryant McGill. NOTICE: You are hereby allowed to be happy, to love yourself, to realise your worth, to believe in great things and to be treated with love and respect…By Thehiyl.com. Let people love you for who you are, because what you are is more than enough for anyone!!…By Positive life.

Wisdom integrated with love recognises potentiality and pursues it with a calm passion…By Harold W. Becker. Unconditional love patiently waits whether you choose to love unconditionally now or later…By The Love Foundation.

When you have love; faith; compassion and hope. You are on your way to a great life!!…By A Positive Life. Life is short. Don't miss opportunities to spend time with the people that you love…By Joel Osteen. Respect yourself enough to walk away from anything that keeps you from loving yourself…By #RehabTime. Raise your vibrations, not your voice, not your defences, to walk away with peace in your heart…By Anna Pereira. When the power of love overcomes the love for power. The world will know peace…By Jimi Hendrix. 14 000 people are having sex right now, 25 000 are kissing. 50 000 are hugging. And you're reading this book…By Baisden Live. Love isn't when you can name a million things you love about the person. Love is when you can't even find words to describe how you feel about them…Unknown.

When they discover the centre of the universe, a lot of people will be disappointed they are not it…By Begin with yes. Remember, anyone can love you when the sun is shinning. It is in the storms where you learn who truly cares for you…By Vincent Happy Mnisi.

A wise woman knows the importance of speaking life into her man. If you love him: believe in him, encourage him and be his peace...By Denzil Washington. Nothing like a love that makes you forget that your worries even exist; your heart deserves a love that erases all your problems...By Trent Shelton. You'll never be enough to somebody who can't recognise your worth. You can't make them see what they choose to stay blind to...By #RehabTime. Letting go doesn't mean you forget the person completely, it just means that you find a way of surviving without them...By Trent Shelton.

The funny thing about a strong woman is that she doesn't need you...She wants you. And if you start slacking she'll be content without you...By Alice 105.9. Never expect...Never assume, Never ask, Never demand. Just let it be. If it's meant to be it will happen...By Where there is love there is life.

No one knows your situation better than you. Do what's best for you and explain it to them later. If they can't love you through it, they weren't meant to be in your life...By Tony Gaskins. Be with someone who is proud to have you...By Change Your Thoughts Today. Relationships last longer when nobody knows your business!...By Bobby V.

Always believe something wonderful is going to happen. Even with all the up's and downs, never take a day for granted. Smile, cherish the little things and remember to hug the ones you really love...By Brigitte Nicale. You'd never invite a thief into your house. So why would you allow, thoughts that steal your joy to make themselves at home in your mind?...By Healing lights. When we detach from our need to hold on, we allow the beauty of our reality to unfold through love...By Love foundation. Learning to appreciate every little thing about me, allow me to love myself all the time, even when I screw up...which is pretty often...By Anna Pereira. Spend life with who makes you happy, not who you have to impress...By Baisden Live.

Negative people don't always occur as negative to me. I like to think their negativity is unfinished hurt and when I can, I love them without labelling them as negative...By Shawne Duperon. Because "Darkness cannot drive out darkness: only light can do that, Hate cannot drive out hate: only love can do that"...By Martin Luther King Jr.

A woman with a beautiful body is good for a night, but a woman with a beautiful mind is good for a lifetime....By Baisden Live. A relationship without trust is like a car without fuel. You stay in it all you want, but it won't go anywhere....By. You might think she wants your car, your cash and gifts. But the right woman wants your time, your smile, your honesty, your efforts and you choosing to put her as a priority...By Nhlanhla Mthobi.

Good Morning, may you cup overflow with peace, love and pure awesomeness today...By Fiona Childs.com. Sometimes the bad things that happen in our lives put us directly on the path to the most wonderful things that will ever happen to us...By Nicole Reed. Love only grows by sharing. You can only have more for yourself by giving it away to others...By Brain Tracy.


If you don't love yourself it will be almost impossible for you to be loved by someone else. You'll give too much and get nothing in return. That's a recipe for self-destruction...By Tony Gaskins. Grant me the strength to focus this week to be mindful and present, to serve with excellence, to be a force of love...By Brendon Burhard. Men don't have to be perfect to make a women happy. All a man really needs to do is love her like he promised when they first dated...By Baisden Live. Don't wait...Tell those you love "I love you"...By Billy Cox Motivation. Treat me like a joke and I will leave you like it's funny...By Baisden Live. Appreciate what you have, before it turns into what you had...Unknown. Real love sometimes means saying Goodbye...By Bryant McGill. Don't love too soon, Don't trust too fast. Don't quit too early. Don't expect to high. Don't talk too much...By Quation.com26807. In our house we are real, we make mistakes we say I'm sorry, we give second chances, We have fun, we give hugs, we forgive, we love, we are family...By Uplifting entertainment. And finally you realise...You can't force it to be something. You can't force consistency, loyalty, or even honesty...You can't force them to keep their word, or to communicate or realise something special is in front of them...By Tami Roman.

Acknowledge something beautiful and something beautiful will acknowledge you...By Bryant McGill. 10 things to remember 1) We are all connected. 2) The more you give the more you get. 3) Love is an infinite resource. 4) You create your own reality. 5) Forgiveness sets you free. 6) Your life has meaning and purpose. 7) Every cloud has a silver lining. 8) The universe supports you. 9) You are doing your best 10) You are incredible...By Lynda Fields

Hate controls everything it touches, but love set everything it touches free...By Bryant McGill. Wrapping paper is easily changed to suite the occasion, but the gift underneath is what's cherished, within should be beautiful thoughtful and filled with love...By Anna Pereira.

You deserve to be with someone who makes you happy. Somebody who doesn't complicate your life. Somebody who won't hurt you...By Grey Anatomy. True love and loyal friends are two of the hardest things to find...By Killian F. Bukutu.

Treat her like you're still trying to win her and that's how you will never lose her...By Basiden Live. Never play with the feelings of others...Because you may win the game but you'll surely lose the person for a lifetime...By lovequotes.com. We cannot go on thinking in hateful ways if we want to bring love to our world...By Wayne Dyer.

Bad relationships are like a bad investment. No matter how much you put into it you'll never get anything out of it. Find someone that's worth investing in...By Sonya Parker. Don't try to fill an emotional gap in your life with spending. No object will ever satisfy your soul...By Vincent Happy Mnisi. The best relationships are the ones you didn't expect to be in, the ones you never saw coming...By Killian F. Bukutu. A strong woman loves, forgives, lets go, tries again and perseveres no matter what...By Women Who Change the World.

Nothing is nicer than having someone who appreciates you in the smallest things...Accepts you in times of hardship. Comforts you when you're troubled. Loves you no matter what and is simply happy for having you in their life...By Steven Aitchison.  Mr Right is going to find you, you don't have hunting skills...By Steve Harvey. Find a heart that will love you at your worst and arms that will hold you at your weakest...Unknown.

Your task is to love each other without wondering if they're worthy. Love is our birthright...By Project-Forgive.com. A great relationship is about two things: First, is appreciating the similarities, and second is respecting the differences...By Womenworking.com. Sometimes the strongest women are the ones who love beyond faults, cry behind closed doors, and fight battles that nobody knows about...By Mediawe Bapps.com. Wherever you go, leave a heart print...By Incredible Joy. You have gotta dance like there's nobody watching, love like you'll never be hurt, sing like there's nobody listening and live like it's heaven on earth...By William W. Durkey.

I don't have an amazing figure or a flat stomach. I'm from being considered a model but I'm me. I eat food. I have curves. I have more fat than I should. I have scars because I have a history. Some people love me, some people like me, some people hate me. I have done good. I have done bad. I don't pretend to be someone I'm not. I am who I am, you can love me or not. I won't change. And if I love you, I do it with my heart. I make no apologies for the way I am...Unknown.

The grass may be greener on the other side of the fence, but yours would be just as green if you took better care of it...By Magan Hillman. The most wonderful places to be in the world are: In someone's thoughts. Someone's prayers...And in someone's heart...By Truthfollowers.com. Let go of unhealthy relationships...By Lynda fields.

Be present, make love, make tea. Avoid small talk, embrace conversation. Buy a plant, water it. Make your bed, make someone's else's bed. Have a smart mouth, and quick wit. Run, Make art, Create. Swim in the ocean, swim in the rain, take chances, ask questions. Make mistakes, learn, know your worth, love fiercely. Forgive quickly. Let go of what doesn't make you happy, Grow...By Paulo Coelho.

Women should be tough, tender, Laugh as much as possible, and live long lives...By Maya Angelou. It's better to be hated for what you are than to be loved for what you are not...By Andre Gide. Never underestimate the importance of having a person in your life who can always make you smile...By incredible Joy. Marry your best friend. I do not say that lightly. Really, truly find the strength, happiest friendship in the person you fall in love with. Someone who speaks highly of you. Someone you can laugh with. The kind of laughs that make your belly ache, and your nose snort. The embarrassing, earnest healing kind of laugh. Which is important. Life is to short not to love someone who lets you be a fool with them. Make sure they are somebody who lets you cry too. Despair will come. Find someone that you want to be there with you through those times. Most importantly, marry the one that makes passion, love and respects you. A love that you will never dilute-even when the waters get deep and dark...By N'tima

Love is not a matter of what happens in life. Its a matter of what's happening in your heart...By Ken Keyes. Love one another and you will be happy. It's as simple and as difficult as that...By Your Inner Sparkle. The power of love is enormous; in fact, every-thing we do in life is either to get love, or to compensate for the lack of love...By Brain Tracy.

Those who see the world through the lens of love are the true Visionaries...By Bryant McGill. The best feeling is when someone appreciates everything about you that someone else took for granted...By Joy of Mom.

Hate controls everything it touches, but love sets everything it touches free...By Bryant McGill. Love one another...By Vincent Happy Mnisi. If you can silence your constant judging, you can have deeper levels of love and friendship with others and yourself...By Bryant McGill. Don't take pride in hanging on in a toxic relationship. There isn't anything noble about being treated worse than a dog and toughing it out. If a person can't be faithful and honest, they don't deserve you...By Tony Gaskins

It is physically possible to lift each other up and hold each other under a starlit sky. Enough to feel the power of the universe enfold us, wrapping us up with simultaneous feelings of love and immensity. Yes, we are only a speck in the whole of things. Yet, our love mingled with the love of others is more immense than we can ever intellectually know...By Doc Klein. I have no fear of losing you, for you aren't an object of my property, or anyone else's. I love you as you are, without attachment, without fears, without conditions, without egoism, trying not to absorb you. I love you freely because I love your freedom, as well as mine...By Baisden Live.

Don't allow yourself t be broken by someone who is insecure, jealous or manipulative. You are worth far more than that...By Anna Pereira. Don't expect her to play he part, if you have other women auditioning for her role...By Baisden Live. A woman has got to love a bad man once or twice in her life to be thankful for the good one...By Mae West. When you get a taste of a real man, the rest of the world never really tastes the same...By KushandWizdom. When a woman is loved correctly, she becomes ten times the woman she was before...Michael Baisden.

Physical attraction are common, but a real mental connection is rare. If you find it, hold onto it...By KushandWizdom. Even strong independent women don't feel like handling things themselves all the time...By Dr Farrah Gray. Having somewhere to go is a home, having someone to love is family, having both is a blessing...By Love covers all. Serving and loving each other is the most powerful form of medicine in the world...By Dr Josh Axe.

The best and most beautiful things in the world cannot be seen or even touched...They must be felt with the heart...By Helen Keller. Speak words of kindness, seed love into the world and encourage others to shine their light. To do this is to create a legacy that will ripple for beyond your lifetime...By Illuminating Souls. Some people cannot love you the way you want to be loved, because they are emotionally and spiritually frozen. They recoil from or avoid affection. You will never meet a deep penetrating gaze from their shallow eyes; only a surface glance. They will touch your hand with their hand, but never with their heart. They will serve your body but not your soul. They can only connect with you through utility, but never passion. They are empty. They are dead inside. They will break your heart if you let them. You will waste your whole life waiting for them to wake-up to the treasure of what you have to offer...By Bryant McGill.

A sense of entitlement is a cancerous thought precess that is void of gratitudes and can be deadly to our relationship...By Steve Maroboli. Two things you will never have to chase; true friends and true love...By Mandy Hale. Please guide me in every moment, in every experience to always choose love in all I think say and do...By Sherri Bishop. We all rejoice in hearing those three little words, "I Love You!" Beneath these three words are another three words "I get you!" It's when we feel truly understood that we feel as if we are being truly loved...By Karen Salmonsohn.

You are the sunshine of my life...By Steve Wonder. We cannot go on thinking in hateful ways if we want to bring love to our world...By Wayne Dyer. Judgement can be found in abundance. Always look for love. Be the giver of love unconditionally...By Anna Pereira.

I choose to honour and respect myself. I have the power within me to decide what I want and who I allow in my heart centre...By Mystic Sounds. In the end, we wont remember the most beautiful face and body. We'll remember-the most beautiful heart and soul...By Team Growing Bolder.com. The woman you pursue is a reflection of you, your ambitions and your level of class or lack thereof...By Pleasure P.

In a relationship honesty and trust must exist, if they don't, there's no point of loving. So if you can't afford to be honest, stay single...By Idle hearts.com There is no love without forgiveness, and there is no forgiveness without love...By Bryant H. McGill. Fact of life: If a girl cries, there maybe thousands reasons. But when a boy cries there is only one reason... "A Girl"...By Laughing Colours. My mum has made me laugh, made me cry, wiped my tears, hugged me tight, watched me succeed, seen me fail, Cheered me on, kept me going strong and drove me crazy. Mom's are a promise from God that you will have a friend forever!...By Pinoy Rap.

Every decision we make is a statement of exactly how much we are loving and valuing ourselves. Be kind to yourself today...By Lynda Fields. The world loves us when we choose to love the world...By Marianne Williamson. It's best to plant seeds in the heart of others, seeds of kindness; seeds of comfort; seeds of love...They always fall on hearty ground...By Living on the Inside. You came to this world to grow and to explore and to touch the miracles and marvels of life. Your suffering needs to be respected. Don't try to ignore the hurt, because the hurt is real. Instead, let the hurt prove there is hope through your healing. Let the hurt soften you instead of hardening you. Let the hurt open you instead of closing you. Let the hurt deliver you to love, and not to hate...By Bryant McGill. As the ocean is never full of water, so is the heart never full of love...By Irie. I never dream of having a perfect relationship, but I always dream of having a long time relationship not for months but for a lifetime...By Social Meens. All life's challenges are the same...just lessons in love...By Eileen Dielesen.

Ten things that money can't buy: 1) Manners 2)Morals 3)Respect 4)Character 5)Common sense 6)Trust 7)Patience 8)Class 9)Integrity 10)Love. Ten old fashioned dating habits we should make cool again. 1) Coming to the door to pick someone up. 2) Trying to dress nicely for a date. 3) Brings flowers or other tokens of affection to the first date. 4) Going dancing that's not grinding on a grimy clubs floor. 5) Straight forwardly asking someone out and not calling it hanging out. 6) Additionally being clear about when you are going steady. 7) Romantic gestures like writing poems. 8) Turning electronics off and just being with one another. 9) The general concept of asking permission for things. 10) Not assuming sex is to be had at any point in time.

Just because the relationship is over doesn't mean your life is too. What you think is the end to your world could be the beginning to your happiness...By

Rehabtime Trent Shelton. Grant me the strength to focus this week, to be mindful and present, to serve with excellence, to be a force of love...By Brendon Burchard.

A daughter needs a good dad to be the standard against which she will judge all men...By Meg Meeker MD. You came to this world to grow and to explore and to touch the miracles and marvels of life. Your suffering needs to be respected, don't to ignore the hurt because hurt is read, instead, let the hurt prove there is hope through your healing. Let the hurt soften you instead of closing you. Let the hurt deliver you to love and not to hate...By Bryant McGill.

For those we love we carry our hopes deeply in our hearts. We anguish when we must watch their painful mistakes. We suffer when they suffer; We rejoice in they joy. Our connection is tempered in both strife and triumph! We struggle, cry, pray and hope for the best. Sometimes we feel taken for granted or unappreciated. But we stand by their side; steady, true and unwavering. For those we love we will carry any burden. Love is the promise that we will be there tomorrow. This is dedicated to those we love and cherish. A promise, today, tomorrow and forever...By Bryant McGill. Don't just say I love you and wait for the world to believe you. Let your gestures show love and witness the world receive and reciprocate it...By Bhavya Gaur.

kindred souls. Live passionately...Respond to every call that excites your spirit...By Rumi. The greatest gift that you can give to others is the gift of unconditional love and acceptance...By Brain Tracy. You don't always have to have the answers. You don't always have to know what to say. Sometimes it's enough to just sit together and share in the quiet moments of the soul...By Laurel Bleadon-Maffei. Attract what you expect, reflect what you desire, become what you respect, mirror what you admire...By Baisden Live. The beauty you see in me is a reflection of you...By Rumi.

Three rules in relationships don't lie, don't cheat and don't make promises you can't keep and don't make promises you can't keep...By Baisden Live. Everything has beauty, but not everyone can see...By Confucius. People think a soul mate is your perfect fit, and that's what everyone wants. But a true soul mate is a mirror, the person who shows you everything that's holding you back, the person who brings you to your own attention so you can change your life, A true soul mate is probably the most important person you'll ever meet, because they tear down your walls and smack you awake...By Elizabeth Gilbert.

A real man makes his lady forget her heart was ever broken...By Dr Farrah Gray. Let your heart be filled with love that energy heals and shift the vibrations of everyone around you...Doreen Virture. Always follow the energy which empowers you leads you to your Truth, makes you feel lighter and connects you to your joy...By Sherri Bishop.

I don't need someone who thinks I'm perfect cause I'm not, I need someone who knows I'll make mistakes and still loves me...By Pleasure P. Love yourself for all you have been, all you are and all you will become...By Liora. Don't be a woman that needs a man...Be a woman a man needs.

They say the people who exhibit the most kindness have experienced a lot of pain. The ones who act like they don't need love, are the ones that need it more. The ones who take care of everyone else's needs are the ones, who needs it most. And the people who smile a lot may be the ones who cry when there is no one is around...By Spirit Science.

The wrong relationship teach you how to recognises the right One when it arrives...By Mandy Hale.We all rejoice in hearing those 3 little words "I love you". Beneath these 3 words are another 3: "I get you". It is when we feel truly Understood that we feel as if we are being truly loved...By Karen Salmansohn

To be fully seen by somebody, and then be loved anyhow...This is a human offering that can border on miraculous...By Elizabeth Gilbert. God made Eve for Adam, not Adam for Eve. Ladies you are the blessing! He who finds a wife finds a good thing!...By Dr Farrah Gray & Proverbs.

WHEN THE POWER OF LOVE OVERCOMES THE LOVE OF POWER THE WORLD WILL KNOW PEACE...BY JIMI HENDRIX. ONCE YOU FALL IN

LOVE, THERE'S NO GOING BACK TO BEING FRIENDS...BY VIRGIN RADIO. LOVE YOURSELF ENOUGH TO CREATE AN ENVIRONMENT IN YOUR LIFE THAT IS CONDUCIVE TO THE NOURISHMENT OF YOUR PERSONAL GROWTH. ALLOW YOURSELF TO LET GO OF THE PEOPLE, THOUGHTS, AND SITUATIONS THAT POISON YOUR WELL-BEING. CULTIVATE A VIBRANT SURROUNDING AND COMMIT YOURSELF TO MAKING CHOICES THAT WILL HELP YOU RELEASE THE GREATEST EXPRESSION OF YOUR UNIQUE BEAUTY AND PURPOSE...BY STEVE MAROBOLI.

STAY SINGLE UNTIL SOMEONE ACTUALLY COMPLIMENTS YOUR LIFE IN A WAY THAT IT MAKES IT BETTER TO NOT BE SINGLE. IF NOT, IT'S NOT WORTH IT...BY KUSHANDWIZDOM. GOOD WOMAN ARE NOT HARD TO FIND, THEY'RE JUST WISER AND HARDER TO PLEASE...DON'T BE A WOMAN THAT NEEDS A MAN...BUT A WOMAN A MAN NEEDS...BY BASIDEN LIVE. WHEN A WOMAN IS LOVED CORRECTLY, SHE BECOMES TEN TIMES THE WOMAN SHE WAS BEFORE...BY BASIDEN LIVE.

PEOPLE THINK A SOUL MATE IS YOUR PERFECT FIT, AND THAT'S WHAT EVERYONE WANTS, BUT A TRUE SOUL MATE IS A MIRROR, THE PERSON WHO SHOWS YOU EVERYTHING THAT'S HOLDING YOU BACK, THE PERSON WHO BRINGS YOU TO YOUR OWN ATTENTION SO YOU CAN CHANGE YOUR LIFE. A TRUE SOUL MATE IS PROBABLY THE MOST IMPORTANT PERSON YOU'LL EVER MEET, BECAUSE THE TEAR DOWN YOUR WALLS AND SMACK YOU AWAKE...BY ELIZABETH GILBERT.

A MAN'S SUCCESS HAS A LOT TO DO WITH THE KIND OF WOMAN HE CHOOSES TO HAVE IN HIS LIFE...BY DANIEL D. SOMETIMES A MAN'S PURPOSE IN A WOMAN'S LIFE IS TO HELP HER BECOME A BETTER WOMAN FOR ANOTHER MAN...BASIDEN LIVE. IT'S NOT A LACK OF LOVE, BUT A LACK OF FRIENDSHIP THAT MAKES UNHAPPY MARRIAGES...BY NIETSCHE.

YOU DON'T MEASURE LOVE IN TIME, YOU MEASURE LOVE IN TRANSFORMATION. SOMETIMES THE LONGEST CONNECTIONS YIELD VERY LITTLE GROWTH, WHILE THE BRIEFEST OF ENCOUNTERS CHANGE EVERYTHING. THE HEART DOESN'T WEAR A WATCH, IT'S TIMELESS. IT DOESN'T CARE HOW LONG YOU KNOW SOMEONE, IT DOESN'T CARE IF YOU HAD 40 YEARS ANNIVERSARY IF THERE IS NO JUICE IN THE CONNECTION. WHAT THE HEART CARES ABOUT IS RESONANCE. RESONANCE THAT OPENS IT, RESONANCE THAT ENLIVENS IT, RESONANCE THAT CALLS IT HOME AND WHEN IT FINDS IT, THE TRANSFORMATION BEGINS...BY JEFF BROWN.

# Chapter 6: FATE&DESTINY

EVERYBODY HAS A DESTINY AND YOU, YES YOU READING THIS BOOK RIGHT NOW! YOU ARE DESTINED FOR GREATNESS BY READING THIS BOOK IT WILL BE ENABLED TO ASPIRE…BY VINCENT HAPPY MNISI. LIFE IS AN ADVENTURE IF YOU ARE UNSURE ABOUT YOUR DESTINY, YOUR AIMS AND HOPES SHOULD SHAPE OUR AMBITIONS AND IT'S NEVER TOO LATE TO LEARN SOMETHING NEW…BY VINCENT HAPPY MNISI. No matter where you are in life right now, know this: God put you on this earth to fulfil the promise He has predestined for your life…By T.D.Jakes. Hardship often prepares ordinary people for an extraordinary destiny…By G. S. Lewis. You are destined for greatness, just keep walking and accomplishing!, but learn to stay away from still people! Still broke, still borrowing, still complaining about their same situation, still hating, still running after the same woman/man, still insecure, still childish, still lying, still cheating, still stuck on stupid, still aren't going to change, still and always will be a headache!…By Vincent Happy Mnisi.

Keep your thoughts positive because your thoughts become your words. Keep your words positive because your words become your behaviour. Keep your Behaviour positive because your behaviour becomes your habits. Your habits become your values, so keep your values positive because your values become your destiny…By Mahatma Gandhi. "On your way to your destiny, there will be times of testing where you don't see anything happening. But you have got to stay in faith and keep believing…By Joel Osteen. I am the master of my fate and the captain of my destiny…by Nelson Mandela.

Your past never has to equal your future, unless you let it…By Billy Cox. Be yourself be honest, do your best. Take care of your family. Treat people with respect. Be a good citizen. Always chase your dreams…By Mel Burchard. Self-belief is the strongest magic…By Claire Mitchell. Doubt kills more dreams than failure ever will...By Kaum Seddick. Aims and dreams are essential in mapping your future...By Vincent Happy Mnisi.

When I am no longer ruled by worries about what others think of me, I am free to be myself...By Lynda Field Life Coach. Go as far as you can see when you get there, you will be able to see farther...By Zig Ziglar.

To make the right choices in life, you have to get in touch with your soul. To do this you need to experience solitude, which most people are afraid of, because in the silence you hear the truth and know the solutions...By Deepak Chopra

Challenges create change, and change promotes Growth! Know that every challenge has an expiration date! No matter how long the night, Day follows!...By Bishop Dale C. Bronner. Sometimes you need to look back, just to find where you dropped your standards. Lost your confidence and started settling for less, than you deserve. Once you discovered that place, pick them back up make peace with that time in your life and march on with your head held high...By Mindful Wishes.

Sometimes when we feel so alone and beat down it's when God steps in to rebuild and mold us more into who we are destined to be...By Jess Vaughn 22. Just because you got a little older doesn't mean you got a little less amazing. In fact with age you have become more wonderful, more beautiful, more dazzling. Never forget, your best years are ahead of you!!!...Unknown. Instead of being discouraged by opposition, be encouraged by it. Knowing that on the other side of that difficulty is a new level of your destiny...By Joel Osteen.

As iron sharpens iron, your difficulties are going to sharpen you...By Joel Osteen. This is your time, this is your moment. You are equipped, empowered and anointed. No weapon formed against you can prosper...By Joel Osteen. As we express our gratitude, we must never forget that the highest appreciation is not to utter words, but to live by them...By John F. Kennedy. Never reply when you are angry, never make a promise when you are happy. Never make a decision when you are sad...By Where there is love there is life.

Don't downgrade your dreams to match your reality, Upgrade your faith to match destiny...By Rickey Smiley. Sometimes all you need is a hundred million dollars…By Sue Fitzmaurice. You'll never know what you're capable of until you take that first step and go for it…By www.livelifehappy.com. Sometimes letting things go is an act of far greater power than defending or hanging on…By Echart Tolle. "Always reach and strive for the next level and never settle for less than your very best"…By Billy Cox. "Ask for what you want and be prepared to get it!"…By Maya Angelou.


Don't lose heart now…Keep going you are much closer than you think…By Lynda Fields. "Only put off what until tomorrow what you are willing to die having left undone"…By Pablo Picasso.

Believe it can be done. When you believe something can be done, really believe, your mind will find the ways to do it. Believing a solution exists paves the way to the solution…By David J. Schwartz. You have unlimited potential, but you must learn to release it to reach your destiny…By Pastor John Hague. Watch your thoughts, for they become words. Watch your words, for they become actions. Watch your actions, for they become habits. Watch your habits, for they become character. Watch your character, for it becomes your destiny…By Zig Ziglar.

If you run after your destiny, you'll escape your history. Get ready to run!…By T.D.Jakes. The road that you are on now differs than the road you were on last year. Things change and can't do the same things on your new journey….By Bishop George G Blommer. Once a person decides which goals he or she wants to accomplish, the process begins. It is therefore important that we set goals….By T.D.Jakes. Those who are for you will not just celebrate in your triumphs, but they will also pray with you through your tribulations…By T.D.Jakes. God has great things planned for you, and his promises are your s to enjoy. Find your place in life through him. Seek him for direction, be willing to do your part and your success in life is guaranteed!…By T.D.Jakes.

I want my children to be independent headstrong people. Just not while I'm raising them….Magic 95.5. Confidence is letting go of blame, moving on from the past. Keeping a sense of humour and radiating positivity. Seeing the good in others and bouncing back from setbacks. Taking a risk and being yourself…By Lynda Fields. The more spiritually aware you become, the more you will focus on your own self and less on others...By Bryant McGill.  Each of us will have our own distinct definition of success because we are unique in our individual dreams and aspirations...By Billy Cox.

Inside you...willing to learn, you are willing to learn from everyone. You learn by doing and you learn by being a part of and co-operating with life. You keep your mind clear and positive and open to new thoughts and creative ideas. You, are ready for change and these changes will take place as they should. You are well centred and this means you take full responsibility for who you are and what you are. You are self-assured about your abilities, about the unlimited power that is within you...By Billy Cox.

Your smile is your logo, your personality is your business card, how you leave others feeling after having an experience with you becomes your trademark...By Lola Berry. Break those habits of negative thinking. Don't believe everything you think! Train your mind so that you believe in yourself and you will increase your confidence and self-esteem...By Lynda fields. To a young heart every-thing's fun...By Charles Dickens. I can do whatever I have to do. I have all the stamina, confidence and courage that I need...By Lynda Fields. Self-belief plus positive emotions plus assertive action will equal Winning outcomes...By Lynda Fields. Are you valuing and supporting yourself or are you sabotaging yourself...By Lynda Fields.

Facing personal truths and purging yourself of addictions or manipulative habits require strength, courage, humility, faith and other qualities of a soul with stamina, because you are not just changing yourself. You are changing your universe. Your soul is a compass, Change one co-ordinate in your spiritual compass and you change your entire life's direction...By Caroline Myss.

Don't give up! It may not look good right now, but be encouraged!...By Dr Dorinda Clarke Cole. To be old and wise you must first be young and stupid...By Alice 105.9 If you plan is for one year plant rice; if you plan is for 10 years, plant trees; If your plan is for 100years educate children...By Confucius.

Success is deciding from the start what end. Result you want and creating the circumstances to realise that result...By Mark Victor Hansen. Say yes to relaxation, Happiness, more fun, confidence, Gratitude, Prosperity, Kindness, enthusiasm, self belief, motivation, creativity, originality and friendship...By Vincent Happy Mnisi.

Be the one who nurtures and builds. Be the one who has an understanding and a forgiving heart one who looks for the best in people. Leave people better than you found them..By Marvin J. Ashton. Pause and remember...If you take the time to look for beauty, you will find it. Open yourself to the beauty you have been missing right before you ...By Senni Young. Don't confuse your path with your destination Just because it's stormy now doesn't mean you aren't headed for sunshine...Unknown. If you don't see yourself as winner, then you cannot perform as a winner...By Zig Ziglar.

The challenge of leadership is to be strong, but not rude; Be kind, but not weak; Be bold, but not bully; Be thoughtful, but not lazy; Be humble, but not timid; Be proud, but not arrogant; Have humour, but without folly...By Jim Rohn. A person can fail many times, but they are not a failure until they give up...By Brain Tracy. The only person you should try to be better than is the person you were yesterday...By Fifi and Dave.

I hope you have some adventures this week. I hope you discover something new. I hope you get to see some beautiful things and I hope you feel peace all the way through...By S. C. Lourie. If you think you're to small to make a difference you haven't spent a night with a Mosquito...An African Proverb. Create a beautiful place inside of yourself and then begin to expand and build outward...By Bryant McGill. I'm not the same soul I once was. A lot has changed. A lot had to change. So you shouldn't expect out of me what I embodied in the past. For that part of me no longer exists...Unknown. Stop allowing other people to dilute or poison your day with their words or opinion. Stand strong in the truth of your beauty and journey through your day without attachment to the validation of others...By Steve Maraboli. Don't judge me by my past. I don't live there anymore...By UPTV.

Looking back to when I wanted something so badly, and didn't get it, I say "What was I thinking?" Now, I see, I had more to experience. If I had gotten what I wanted back then, succeeding would have ended in failure. Dreams come and sit with you when the timing is right...By Anna Pereira. I dream, I do, I become...By Charles F. Glassman MD. If you settle for just anything, you'll never know what you're truly worthy of...By Necole Stephens.

I am grateful for my life. The past is a blessing because it is my teacher. The future is a blessing because it is my opportunity...By Mystic Sounds. Never restart a journey and use the same road that failed you before...By Dennis E. Adonis. Good enough is not your destiny. You are a child of God. You were created fir excellence...By I Am a Child of God. I choose to honour and respect myself. I have the power within me to decide what I want, and how I want to live...By Mystic Sounds. Worrying is like praying for what you don't want...Unknown.

We are all visitors to this time, this place. We are just passing through. Our purpose here is to observe, to learn, to grow, to love...and then we return home...An Australian Aboriginal Proverb. Regardless of your past, your tomorrow is a clean slate...By Zig Ziglar. We are what we repeatedly do. Excellence, therefore, is not an act but a habit...By Aristotle. I am open to receive the possibilities and potential, I am destined for. Those things that I am not even aware of yet, on my path, are Great and Glorious...Affirm....By Anna Pereira.

Optimism is the faith that leads to achievement. Nothing can be done without hope and confidence in achieving our dreams....By Vincent Happy Mnisi. The promise of untold possibilities is whispered into the heart of every tomorrow...By Sue Krebs. What is coming will make sense of what is happening. Let God finish his work...By A woman of faith. Each day, focus your attention on what you want. Each day, take one step that will bring you closer to it. All things are possible! The key is to identify it, claim it for yourself, and believe that you are worthy to have it...By Iyanla Vanzant. Change can be beautiful when we are brave enough to evolve with it, and change can be brutal when we fearfully resist...By Bryant McGill. How often I found where I should be going only by setting out for somewhere else...By Bucksminsiter Fuller.

You alone are the judge of your worth and your goal is to discover infinite worth in yourself, no matter what anyone else thinks...By Deepok Chopra. You don't pay the price for success. You pay the price for failure. You enjoy the benefits of success...By Zig Ziglar.

Mathematics of life-life is laughter multiplied by love which subtracts hate which in-turn equals Happiness...By Bryant McGill. The secret of getting ahead is getting started...By Brain Tracy. Your imagination is a gateway to the greater expanse of wisdom available to you. Dreams beyond this moment. Travel beyond what is present now, Allow yourself to bathe in the mystical the joyous and the creative potential that calls forth from your soul...By Laurel Bleadon-Maffei. Imagination is good...dream up your future and then work towards it... you will soon attain it...By Vincent Happy Mnisi.

There is always time each day to progress in some way towards our dreams, even if just in a small way. Believing otherwise is to hand over our life agenda to a small thinking world that could barely fathom our true hearts and power...By Brendon Burchard. Over and over, I have found that the key to success are a single piece of information, a single idea at the right time, in the right situation, and change your life. I have also learned that the great truths are simple...By Brain Tracy. I am stronger because I had to be, I'm smarter because of my mistakes, happier because of the sadness I've known, and now wiser because I learned...By Curriano.com

B bold and courages, respectful and courteous but whatever you do...stay true to you....By Kenni Gambo. Believe in your ability to co-create your dreams with the universe. The future is not yet determined. You seed your future each and everyday. What do you desire? Intentionally take one action, no matter how small towards your dream each day...By Laurel Bleadon-Maffei. One's destination is never a place but rather a new way of looking at things ...By Henry Miller. I release the past. Today is a new day. I can begin again...By Lynda Fields. Every-thing will be all right, in the end. If it's not right, it just means that it's not the end...By John Lenon.

I am stronger because I had to be, I'm smarter because of my mistakes, happier because of the sadness I've known and now wiser because I learned...By Curiano.com. Your life only gets better when you get better...By Brain Tracy. Your day is only as good as you make it, make it great...By Vicki Yohe. To be successful, raise your standards and change your rituals!...By Anthony Robbins.

Experience the light by closing your eyes and feeling it...By Anna Pereira. If you have struggled today and found it hard, remember tomorrow is another day and another chance. I am with you...By Graham Kean. The best day of your life is the one on which you decide your life is your own. No apologies or excuses and you alone are responsible for the quality of it. This is the day your life really begins...By Bob Moawad.

The Raw truth: You will never be happy unless you love yourself. Happiness is not found in words or gifts from others. Happiness is not found in lives of perfection. Happiness comes from gratitude for what we have, hope that there will always be enough and love for all things. The key, if you can't feel that way, something needs to change...By Anna Pereira.

Success is realising a worthy ideal...not in the eyes if society, because success means different things to different people. Only consider what is worthy and important to you, never compare yourself to anyone else, just learn from other be the best you, that you can be...By Anthony Robbins. As you rest...May all of heaven conspire together on your behalf to prepare a great tomorrow with fresh open doors...By Sandi Krakowski. When we step out of our comfort zones, we step into the Magic!!!...By Lynda Fields. Your suffering is not senseless. Your suffering is here to help you unfold and to awaken into compassion, love and strength...By Bryant McGill.

Don't ever put your happiness in someone's else's hands, they'll drop it. They'll drop it every time...By Christopher Barzak. Close some doors today. Not because of pride, incapacity or arrogance, but simply because they lead you nowhere...By Paulo Coelho. Courage is not the absence of fear, it is the ability to face it, overcome it and finish your job...By Billy Cox. The 3 C's in Life: Choice, Chance and Change. You must make the choice to take the chance if you want anything in life to change...By Zig Ziglar. Your thoughts will drive your results, your success and even your destiny...Billy Cox. Sometimes adversity is what you need to face in-order to become successful...By Zig Ziglar. There is no rush. The right answer, the right opportunity and the right decision always comes at the right time...By Shawne Duperon. Within you you will find everything you need to be complete...By Bryant McGill.

I have absolutely no desire to fit in...By Incredible Joy. The past is your lesson, the present is your gift. The future is your motivation. Learn from Yesterday, live for today. Hope for tomorrow...Unknown. If you are struggling right now, may you remember that tomorrow is another day and that there is always hope. May you remember what a gift you are to the world and that you remember that even when you feel lonely, you are never truly alone and that you are surrounded by many Angles who love you beyond measure. You are in my prayers...By Anna Taylor.

I am only me, but I am one, I cannot do everything, but I can do something. And I will not let what I cannot do interfere with what I can do...By Edward Everett Hale. Even in the face of tribulation and persecution, when you are doing what you are destined to do, they will increase your joy...By T. B. Joshua.

No matter how far in the distance your dream, for as long as you cam smell it's fragrance on the breeze, keep moving towards it...By Anna Pereira. No matter who you are or what you do, the ground is always shaky. And the really good news is that shaky ground is fertile ground for spiritual growth and awakening...By Pema Chodron.

It is never to late to make a fresh start...By Lynda Fields. I am in charge of how I feel, and today I am choosing happiness...By Sifiso E. Ntuli. I choose to live by choice not chance; to make changes, not excuses; to be motivated, not manipulated; To be useful, not used; To excel, not compete. I choose self-esteem, not self pity. I choose to listen to my inner voice, to not the random opinion of others...By Incredible Joy.

You will never be happy if you chase money all your life. Find real joy through giving and serving others...By Dave Ramsey. When you are connected to your destiny, nothing can stop you!"...By T. B. Joshua. When you discover your destined assignment, you discover yourself...You discover your future...By T.B. Joshua. When you are doing what you are destined to do, even though you pass through valley of the shadow of death, you will fear no one, If you are not doing what you are destined to do, the shadow will quench you...By T. B. Joshua.

Sometimes the hardest thing and the right thing are the same...By Baisden Live. Do your thing and don't care if they like it or not...By Tina Fey. When the voices of doubt start whispering, turn up the volume of faith and listen to your heart...By Bryant McGill. Today I'm not gonna mess with causes me stress...By Anna Pereira. Our Ancestors knew, we need to understand our past to make sense of our future. Hence Bob Marley sang "If you know your history the you will know where you are coming from".If you believe in what you are doing why should disappointment separate you from it? If you believe in your marriage, why should crisis lead to divorces. If you believed in your business, why should failure lead to you abandon it...By T. B. Joshua. We cannot change a pain-filled past. What we can do is change how it affects us. The past has already been written, but we have the power to write the future based on self-support and respect. We can write a future full of strength, peace, wealth and love. All we have to do is what is right now...By Iyanla Vanzant.

Giving up is not the answer, neither is giving in. Stand your ground. There is a way of doing that without having to be combative. There is way of hanging on to your true self, and demonstrating it, without resorting to aggression. But giving up and giving in is not the way, simply and quietly claim your rights to be you is the way. You know exactly why you are reading this book today??...By Neale Donald Walsch and Vincent Happy Mnisi.

Make me strong in spirit, Courageous in action and Gentle of heart. Let me act in wisdom, Conquer my fear and doubt. To discover my own hidden gifts. To Meet others with compassion. To become a source of healing energies and to face each day with hope and joy...Unknown and Vincent Happy Mnisi.

I wanna live like I have nothing to lose. And love like I have nothing to gain and to run like I have nothing to chase. And to dream like every-thing is possible. I wanna speak like I have nothing to fear and look in your eyes like I have nothing to hide. And to dance like I have nothing to worry about. And to embrace being alive like I only have today. I wanna spread my wings like I've never fallen short. And open my heart wide like I've never doubted at all. And breathe in my soul like I am born again in each and every new moment because we are, Because we all are!...By S. C. Lourie.

No body else gets to live your life. You're the artist. Paint your picture. Dream your own masterpiece into being...By Anna Taylor. Wishing you a day filled with happy surprises and blessings galore!...By Incredible joy. Be a witness, not a judge. Focus on yourself, not others. Listen to your heart not the crowd...Unknown. Self honesty is the greatest honesty because it leads to all significant change...By Billy Cox. All that you are meant to become begins where you're standing in this very moment...By Sherri Bishop. The man who does more than he is paid, will soon be paid for more than he does...By Vincent Happy Mnisi. If you ever find yourself in the wrong story, leave!...By Mo Willems. Beware of destination addictions...a preoccupation with the idea that happiness is in the next place, the next job and with the next partner. Until you give up the idea that happiness is somewhere else, it will never be where you are...By Mankind Project. Starting over requires no explanations to anyone, requires no specific dates, requires nothing more than you saying "It time"...By Anna Pereira.

Forget all the reasons why it won't work and believe the reason why it will...By Joy of Dad. Be patient when it seems things are not going right and may never be right again, Accept that what is yours will come to you in the right way at just the right moment...By Iyanla Vanzant. Imagine with all your mind. Believe with all your heart. Achieve with all your might...By Necole Stephens. When you find yourself doubting how far you can go, just remember how far you've already come...By Master Shift. Success is not a destination, it's a journey...By Zig Ziglar.

Stop blaming and start being! We attract who we are. If you don't like something in your life, look only at who you are. Who you are is why you choose the friends and situations in your life. Who you are is why you choose the friends and situations in your life. Who you are is why you choose poorly, or fail to choose wisely. STOP BEING A VICTIM!!!...BY Bryant McGill.

Remember this, my darling....remember this. What you achieve on earth is only a small part of the deal. If there's a secret I could whisper and that you could keep it would be that it's all inside you already. Every single thing you need. Earth is just a stop over. A kinder game. Make it a star game. If I could

give you a gift, it would be to find the glory inside yourself, beyond the roles and the drama, so you can dance the dance of the game of life with a little more rhythm, a little more abandon, a little more shaking-those-hips...By Annie Kagan.

The process of finding happiness within ones own self may be difficult and slow but it cannot be found anywhere else...By Swami Parthasarthy. Stay focused, follow your heart. Be compassionate...By Brendon Burchard. Miracles come in moments. Be ready and willing...By Wayne Dyer. Don't let happiness depend on something you may lose...By C. S. Lewis.

SOMETIMES WHEN THINGS ARE FALLING APART, THEY MAY ACTUALLY BE FALLING INTO PLACE...BY HEALING LIGHT. SOMETIMES THE BAD THINGS THAT HAPPEN IN OUR LIVES PUT US DIRECTLY ON THE PATH TO THE BEST THINGS THAT WILL EVER HAPPEN TO US...BY THE MASTER SHIFT. THINGS WORK BEST FOR THOSE WHO MAKE THE BEST OF HOW THINGS WORK OUT...BY BRAIN TRACY. THERE IS ALWAYS, ALWAYS SOMETHING TO BE GRATEFUL FOR...BY POWER OF POSITIVITY. WE EACH HAVE A PLACE AND A PURPOSE IN THE CIRCLE OF LIFE...BY HEART AND SOUL MATTERS.

EVERYTHING MAY WELL HAPPEN FOR A REASON BUT THAT DOESN'T MEAN EVERYTHING MAKES SENSE. LIFE IS VERY OFTEN A MYSTERY AND SOMETIMES ACCEPTING THAT IS THE BEST WE CAN DO...BY ANNA TAYLOR.

MORNING PRAYER: LORD TODAY I JUST THANK YOU FOR EVERYTHING IN MY LIFE GOOD AND BAD...THEY ARE ALL PART OF WHICH I AM AND THEY ARE ALSO PART OF YOUR PLAN...BY JESS VAUGHN22. DON'T PUT A ? QUESTION MARK WHERE THERE SHOULD BE A PERIOD...FULL STOP. WHEN SOMETHING IS OVER, MOVE ON TO THE NEXT CHAPTER...JOEL OSTEEN. PEACE ISN'T THE ABSENCE OF TROUBLE, ITS KNOWING THAT GOD IS RIGHT THERE WITH YOU IN THE MIDST OF THE TROUBLE...BY JOEL OSTEEN. PEACE IS A WAY OF BEING WITHIN THAT BRINGS MORE PEACE TO THE WORLD THROUGHOUT ...BY HAROLD W. BECKER. IF YOU ARE GOING THROUGH DIFFICULT TIMES KEEP TRUSTING GOD HE KNOWS HOW TO BLESS YOU IN UNEXPECTED WAYS!...BY LIFE IS POSSIBLE. CONFORMITY IS THE FAILER OF FREEDOM AND THE ENEMY OF GROWTH...BY JOHN F. KENNEDY. I THINK IT'S BETTER TO DO RIGHT, EVEN IF WE SUFFER IN SO DOING, THAN TO INCUR THE REPROACH OF OUR CONSCIENCES AND POSTERITY...BY ROBERT E. LEE.

WHAT WAS YOUR BIGGEST WORRY FIVE YEARS AGO? HOW DO YOU FEEL ABOUT IT NOW? ANY THOUGHTS? BY POSITIVEATMOSPHERE.COM. A LITTLE KNOWLEDGE THAT ACTS IS WORTH INFINITELY MORE THAN MUCH KNOWLEDGE THAT IS IDLE...BY KHADIL GIBNOT.

WHAT LIES BEHIND US AND WHAT LIES AHEAD OF US ARE TINY MATTERS COMPARED TO WHAT LIVES WITHIN US...BY HENRY DAVID THOREAU. WHEN THEY KNOW YOU'LL SETTLE FOR LESS, DON'T EXPECT TO GET MORE...BY #REHABITIME. SOMETIMES THINGS HAVE TO GO VERY WRONG BEFORE THEY CAN BE RIGHT...BY#REHABBTIME. ACCEPT...THEN ACT. WHATEVER THE PRESENT MOMENT CONTAINS, ACCEPT IT AS IF YOU HAD CHOSEN IT. ALWAYS WORK WITH IT, NOT AGAINST IT...BY ECKHART TOLLE. ACCEPT WHAT IS, LET GO OF WHAT

WAS AND HAVE FAITH IN WHAT WILL BE...BY WWW.LIVWLIFEHAPPY.COM

TRAVEL, AS MUCH AS YOU CAN. AS FAR AS YOU CAN, AS LONG AS YOU CAN. LIFE'S NOT MEANT TO BE LIVED IN ONE PLACE...BY WISDOM ONE DAY, YOU'LL BE JUST A MEMORY FOR SOME PEOPLE. DO YOUR BEST TO BE A GOOD ONE...BY VINCENT HAPPY MNISI. THE GREATEST GIFT YOU CAN GIVE SOMEONE IS YOUR TIME. BECAUSE WHEN YOU GIVE YOUR TIME. YOU ARE GIVING A PORTION OF YOUR LIFE THAT YOU WILL NEVER GET BACK...BY WHERE THERE IS LOVE THERE IS LIFE. THE BEST TIME TO PLANT A TREE WAS 20 YEARS AGO. THE SECOND BEST TIME IS NOW...A CHINESE PROVERB.

WE ARE NOT ALWAYS GUARANTEED PERFECT OR EVEN EASY DAYS. IN FACT, SOME OF THE MOST OPTIMISTIC PEOPLE I KNOW HAVE DEALT WITH SOME EXTRA ORDINARY CHALLENGES AND ENDURED MANY DARK DAYS. SON DON'T THINK EASY DAYS ARE ALWAYS A GOOD WAY TO JUDGE PROGRESS OR SUCCESS. GETTING UP AND OUT THE DOOR ON THOSE DIFFICULT DAYS AND TAKING A STEP FORWARD DESPITE THE CHALLENGES IS A MUCH MORE ACCURATE BAROMETER...BY PAUL S. BOYNTON. GOOD THINGS COME TO THOSE WHO BELIEVE, BETTER THINGS COME TO THOSE WHO ARE PATIENT AND THE BEST THINGS COME TO THOSE WHO DON'T GIVE UP...BY WISDOM. LIFE IS SHORT, DON'T WASTE IT BEING SAD. BE WHO YOU ARE, BE HAPPY, BE FREE, BE WHATEVER YOU WANT TO BE...BY WISDOM

NOTHING EVER GOES AWAY UNTIL IT TEACHES US WHAT WE NEED TO KNOW...BY PEMA CHODRON. WHEN WE MAKE A CHANGE, ITS SO EASY TO INTERPRET OUR UNSETTLEDNESS AS UNHAPPINESS, OR OUR UNHAPPINESS AS A RESULT OF HAVING MADE THE WRONG DECISION. OUR MENTAL AND EMOTIONAL STATES FLUCTUATE MADLY WHEN WE MAKE BIG CHANGES IN OUR LIVES. SOME DAYS WE COULD TIGHT-ROPE WALK ACROSS MANHATTAN AND OTHER DAYS WE ARE TO WEARY TO

CLEAN OUT TEETH. THIS IS NORMAL. THIS IS NATURAL. THIS IS CHANGE...BY JEANETTE WINTERSON.

DO THE LITTLE THINGS OTHERS WONT TO HAVE THE BIG THINGS OTHER DON'T...BY BILLY COX YOUR STRUGGLE IS YOUR STRENGTH. IF YOU CAN RESIST BECOMING NEGATIVE, BITTER OR HOPELESS IN TIME, YOUR STRUGGLES WILL GIVE YOU EVERYTHING...BY BRYANT MCGILL.

IF YOU WANT SOMETHING YOU NEVER HAD, YOU HAVE TO DO SOMETHING YOU'VE NEVER DONE...BY BILLY COX. "IT'S IMPOSSIBLE" SAID PRIDE. "IT'S RISKY" SAID EXPERIENCE. "IT'S POINTLESS" SAID REASON. "GIVE IT A TRY" WHISPERED THE HEART...BY BILLY COX. YOU CAN DO IT! JUST DO IT...BY LYNDA FIELDS AND NIKE.

CHIVALRY NEVER DIED. THE GENTLEMAN IN MOST MEN DID. BEING MALE IS A MATTER OF BIRTH, BEING A MAN IS A MATTER OF AGE, BUT BEING A GENTLEMAN IS A MATTER OF CHOICE...BY GRANT WILSON. WHEN I STOP COMPARING MYSELF WITH OTHERS I AM FREE TO STAND IN MY OWN LIGHT...BY LYNDA FIELDS. BANKRUPTCY MAY SEEM LIKE AN EASY WAY OUT OF DEBT, BUT IT WON'T FIX THE BEHAVIOUR THAT GOT YOU THERE IN THE FIRST PLACE...BY DAVE RAMSEY. POSITIVE CHANGE HAPPENS WHEN YOU: CHANGE YOUR THOUGHTS, CHANGE YOUR FEELINGS AND CHANGE YOUR ACTIONS...BY LYNDA FIELDS. I HAVE TO HAVE QUIET TIME. IT'S HOW I'M ABLE TO APPRECIATE BEAUTY...BY SUE FITZMAURICE. SOMETIMES, SIMPLY BY SITTING, THE SOUL COLLECTS WISDOM...BY LEN MOVERB. SOMETIMES WE HAVE TO LET GO OF WHAT'S KILLING US, EVEN IF IT'S KILLING US TO LET GO ...BY THE QUEENS CODE. ALWAYS BELIEVE THAT SOMETHING WONDERFUL TO ABOUT TO HAPPEN...BY BASIDEN LIVE

WITHOUT MY CELL PHONE, I WOULDN'T: 1) KNOW WHAT TIME IT IS. 2) BE ABLE TO SOLVE A MATHS QUESTIONS. 3)KNOW A SINGLE PHONE NUMBER. 4) KNOW THE DATE. 5)BE ABLE TO TEXT MY FRIEND WHEN

I'M AT THEIR HOUSE. 6) TAKE A SNAP SHOT A PICTURE-PERFECT TIME.  7) BE ABLE TO WAKE UP FROM AN ALARM IN THE MORNING. 8) FIND MY WAY IN THE DARK. MY MORNING AFFIRMATIONS... "TODAY IS AN INCREDIBLE DAY! SUCCESS, PROSPERITY AND ABUNDANCE IN MANY DIFFERENT FORMS HAVE NATURALLY FOUND THEIR WAY INTO MY LIFE TODAY. I GRATEFULLY ENJOY  THEIR MANIFESTATIONS THROUGHOUT MY DAY AND HAPPILY SHARE THESE BLESSING OF ABUNDANCE WITH MANY OTHERS IN ORDER TO BRING HAPPINESS TO THEIR DAY AS WELL. I AM HAPPY; I AM HEALTHY; I AM WEALTHY; I AM SECURE; I AM WORTHY; I AM POSITIVE; I AM BLESSED; I AM GRATEFUL; I AM BEAUTIFUL;  I AM CONFIDENT; I AM COURAGEOUS; I AM EXCITED ABOUT TODAY...BY

BY SOWING  SEEDS OF POSITIVITY IN THOUGHT AND ACTION, YOU WILL REAP POSITIVE OUTCOMES. WE REAP WHAT  WE SOW!...BY LYNDA FIELDS. CHOICES, CHANCES, CHANGES. YOU MUST MAKE A CHOICE  TO TAKE A CHANCE OR YOUR  LIFE WILL EVER CHANGE..UNKNOWN.


THE UNIVERSE IS ALWAYS SPEAKING TO US...SENDING US LITTLE MESSAGES, CAUSING COINCIDENCES AND SERENDIPITIES, REMINDING US TO STOP, TO LOOK AROUND TO BELIEVE IN SOMETHING ELSE SOMETHING MORE...BY NANY THAYER.

THE FIRST 40 YEARS OF CHILDHOOD ARE ALWAYS THE HARDEST...UNKNOWN. EARTH PROVIDES ENOUGH TO SATISFY EVERY MAN'S NEEDS, BUT NOT EVERY MAN'S GREED...BY MAHATMA GANDHI. EVERY POSSIBILITY ALREADY EXISTS AND ARE ALREADY HAPPENING RIGHT NOW...TIME IS AN ILLUSION THAT WE CREATE FOR OURSELVES, THROUGH CONNECTING THESE STRINGS OF POTENTIAL MOMENTS. EVERYTHING AND EVERY EXPERIENCE IS AVAILABLE TO EVERYONE AT ALL TIMES...BY SPIRIT SCIENCE.

SPEND YOUR ENERGY ON THINGS THAT MAKE A DIFFERENCE...BY M RUSSELL BALLARD. THE BEST WAY TO PREDICT THE FUTURE IS TO INVENT IT...BY BRAIN TRACY. LET THE PAST BE THE PAST IT'S TIME...BY BRYANT MCGILL. NO MATTER HOW YOU FEEL. GET UP, DRESS UP, SHOW UP, AND NEVER GIVE UP...BY VINCENT HAPPY MNISI. START WHERE YOU ARE...USE WHAT YOU HAVE, DO WHAT YOU CAN...BY ARTHUR ASHE. TRUST YOUR GUT, IT HAS NO ULTERIOR MOTIVES...BY ANNA PEREIRA. HALF OF ME IS FILLED WITH BURSTING WORDS AND HALF OF ME IS PAINFULLY SHY. I CRAVE SOLITUDE YET ALSO CRAVE PEOPLE. I WANT TO OUR LIFE AND LOVE INTO EVERYTHING, YET ALSO NURTURE MYSELF CARE AND GO GENTLY. I WANT TO LIVE WITHIN THE RUSH OF PRIMAL INTUITIVE DECISION, YET ALSO WISH TO SIT AND CONTEMPLATE. THIS IS MESSINESS OF LIFE- THAT WE ALL CARRY MULTITUDES, SO MUST SIT WITH THE SHIFTS WE ARE COMPLICATED CREATURES, AND THE BALANCE COMES FROM THAT UNDERSTANDING. BE OKAY WITH THE FLOW. BE WATER, FLEXIBLE AND SOFT. SUBTLY POWERFUL AND OPEN. WILD AND SERENE. ABLE TO CARRY AND ACCEPT ALL CHANGES, YET STILL LED BY THE PULL OF STEADY TIDES. IT IS ENOUGH ..BY VICTORIA ERICKSON.

WE CHANGE OUR NEGATIVE BELIEFS ABOUT OURSELVES BY TRAINING OUR MINDS TO BELIEVE POSITIVE THINGS INSTEAD...BY LYNDA FIELDS. MY PAST HAS NOT DEFINED ME, DESTROYED ME, DETERRED ME OR DEFEATED ME. IT HAS ONLY STRENGTHENED ME...BY DR STEVE MARBOLI. POSITIVE CHANGES ARE HAPPENING IN MY LIFE RIGHT NOW!I ONLY NEED TO FOCUS THEM AND APPRECIATE THEM. WHEN I CAN DO THIS I OPEN THE DOOR TO MORE AND MORE POSITIVE EXPERIENCES...BY LYNDA FIELDS. TRAIN YOUR MIND , IF YOU FOCUS ON YOUR PROBLEMS YOU WILL CREATE EVEN MORE PROBLEMS. BUT IF YOU FOCUS ON POSSIBILITIES INSTEAD YOU WILL CREATE POSITIVE OPPORTUNITIES...BY LYNDA FIELDS

WHEN YOUR LIGHT BURNS BRIGHT FROM WITHIN, EVEN THE BLIND CAN SEE YOUR GLOW!!...BY ANNA PAREIRA. YOU DON'T HOLD A GRUDGE...IT HOLD YOU. IT HOLDS YOU IN A SELF IMPOSED PRISON OF PAIN. LET IT GO, BECAUSE UNTIL YOU DO YOU ARE BLIND AND YOU CANNOT SEE WITH YOUR SPIRITUAL EYES...UPGRADE YOURSELF CONSTANTLY...BY SUE FITZMAURICE.

THE TONGUE IS SMALL THING, BUT WHAT ENORMOUS DAMAGE IT CAN DO...JAMES 3:4 (TLB). BEING POWERFUL IS REALISING THAT YOU DON'T HAVE TO HIDE ANYTHING FROM ANYONE...BY GENEEN ROTH. HOW STRANGE THAT THE NATURE OF LIFE IS CHANGE, YET THE NATURE OF HUMAN BEINGS IS TO RESIST CHANGE AND HOW IRONIC THAT THE DIFFICULT TIMES WE FEAR MIGHT RUIN US ARE THE VERY ONES THAT CAN BREAK US OPEN AND HELP US BLOSSOM INTO WHO WE WERE MEANT TO BE...BY ELIZABETH LESSER.

OFTEN WHEN YOU THINK YOU'RE AT THE END OF SOMETHING, YOU'RE AT THE BEGINNING OF SOMETHING ELSE...BY FRED ROGERS. HAVE FAITH. A MIRACLE IS TRANSFORMING YOU TO YOUR HIGHEST SELF!...BY BRYANT MCGILL. ACCEPT THE APOLOGY YOU NEVER RECEIVED...BY PROJECT FORGIVE.COM. DREAMS DO COME TRUE FOR THOSE WHO DARE TO BELIEVE IN THEMSELVES...BY BRYANT MCGILL.

I PROMISE MYSELF TO TALK HEALTH, HAPPINESS AND PROSPERITY TO EVERY PERSON I MEET...BY CHRISTIAN D. LARSON. UNTIL YOU HEAL THE WOUNDS OF YOUR PAST, YOU ARE GOING TO BLEED. YOU CAN BANDAGE THE BLEEDING WITH FOOD, WITH ALCOHOL, WITH DRUGS, WITH WORK, WITH CIGARETTES, WITH SEX; BUT EVENTUALLY, IT WILL ALL OOZE THROUGH AND STAIN YOUR LIFE. YOU MUST FIND THE STRENGTH TO OPEN THE WOUNDS, STICK YOUR HANDS INSIDE, PULL OUT THE CORE OF THE PAIN THAT IS HOLDING YOU IN YOUR PAST, THE MEMORIES AND MAKE PEACE WITH THEM...BY LYANLA VANZANT. SURRENDER TO WHAT IS, LET GO OF WHAT WAS. HAVE

FAITH IN WHAT WILL BE...BY SONIA RICOFI. WE ARE HERE, IT SEEMS TO BE TRANSFORMED AND TRANSFORMED AGAIN AND AGAIN AND AGAIN...BY MICHAEL CUNNINGHAM.

THE TRUTH IS THAT, EVEN WHEN I AM NOT OKEY. I STILL FEEL BLESSED AND GRATEFUL...BY MYSTIC SOUNDS. LESSON OF TIME...KARMA...WHEN A BIRD IS ALIVE IT EATS ANTS. WHEN A BIRD IS DEAD...ANTS EAT THE BIRD. TIME AND CIRCUMSTANCES CAN CHANGE AT ANY TIME...DON'T DEVALUE OR HURT ANYONE INN LIFE. YOU MAY BE POWERFUL TODAY. BUT REMEMBER TIME IS MORE POWERFUL THAN YOU! ONE TREE MAKES A MILLION MATCH STICKS...ONLY ONE MATCH STICK IS NEEDED TO BURN A MILLION TREES...SO BE GOOD AND DO GOOD...BY HAPA.

A PERSON'S MIND IS SO POWERFUL. WE CAN INVENT, CREATE, EXPERIENCE AND DESTROY THINGS WITH THOUGHTS ALONE...BY BRAIN TRACY. THE MOST AUTHENTIC THING ABOUT US IS OUR CAPACITY TO CREATE, TO OVERCOME, TO ENDURE, TO TRANSFORM, TO LOVE AND TO BE GREATER THAN OUR SUFFERING...BY BEN OKRI. IT'S IMPOSSIBLE" SAID PRIDE. "IT'S RISKY" SAID EXPERIENCE. "IT'S POINTLESS" SAID REASON. "GIVE IT A TRY" WHISPERED THE HEART...BY BILLY COX.

YOU CAN DO IT! JUST DO IT...BY LYNDA FIELDS AND NIKE.

FORGIVE OTHERS, NOT BECAUSE THEY DESERVE IT BUT BECAUSE IT WILL GIVE YOU PEACE...BY LESSONS LEARNED IN LIFE. IF YOU NEVER CHANGE YOUR MIND, WHY HAVE ONE?...BY EDWARD DE BONO. WHEN THINGS ARE GETTING YOU DOWN AND DAYS ARE FEELING DIFFICULT. PAUSE. PAUSE, TAKE A DEEP BREATH AND THINK UPON THE TROUBLES YOU DON'T HAVE. PAUSE. TAKE A DEEP BREATH AGAIN AND REMEMBER THE LITTLE GRACES YOU DO. NEVER FORGET; THINGS COULD ALWAYS BE WORSE AND IT WILL ALWAYS GET BETTER...BY S.

C. LOUISE. "DON'T DESPAIR WHEN DISSATISFACTION STRIKES...THIS MIGHT SIMPLY BE A NEW TRANSITION FOR YOU. SOMETIMES WHEN THINGS DON'T LOOK GREAT IT CAN BE A SIGN THAT WE HAVE BEEN WORKING HARD ON OUR PERSONAL DEVELOPMENT. WHEN WE CHANGE ON THE INSIDE THEN OUR OUTSIDE CONDITIONS MIGHT NOT MATCH OUR NEW INNER REALITY. CHECK IF THIS IS TRUE FOR YOU, PERHAPS MATCH YOUR NEW ATTITUDES AND EXPECTATIONS...BY LYNDA FIELDS.

EDUCATE A BOY AND YOU EDUCATE AN INDIVIDUAL. EDUCATE A GIRL AND YOU EDUCATE A COMMUNITY...AN AFRICAN PROVERB. TIME DISCOVERS TRUTH...A LATIN PROVERB. FAITH PLUS ACTION EQUALS TRANSFORMATION...BY CHARLES .F GLASSMAN MD. THE SECRET OF CHANGE IS TO FOCUS ALL OF YOUR ENERGY, NOT FIGHTING THE OLD...BUT ON BUILDING THE NEW....BY SOCRATES YOU CANNOT CHANGE WHAT YOU REFUSE TO CONFRONT...BY SOBRIETY BY THE GRACE OF GOD. EVERYTHING AND EVERYONE IS YOUR TEACHER...BY BRYANT MCGILL.

EACH DAY, FOCUS YOUR ATTENTION ON WHAT YOU WANT. EACH DAY, TAKE ONE STEP THAT WILL BRING YOU CLOSER TO IT. ALL THINGS ARE POSSIBLE! THE KEY IS TO IDENTIFY IT, CLAIM IT FOR YOURSELF, AND BELIEVE THAT YOU ARE WORTHY TO HAVE IT...IYANLA VANZANT.

FINISH EACH DAY AND BE DONE WITH IT. YOU HAVE DONE WHAT YOU COULD. SOME BLUNDERS AND ABSURDITIES NO DOUBT CREPT IN, FORGET THEM AS SOON AS YOU CAN. TOMORROW IS A NEW DAY. YOU SHALL BEGIN IT SERENELY AND WITH TOO HIGH A SPIRIT TO BE ENCUMBERED WITH YOUR OLD NONSENSES...BY RALPH WALDO EMERSON.

WHEN ONE DOOR CLOSES, ANOTHER OPENS, BUT WE OFTEN LOOK SO LONG AND SO REGRETFULLY UPON THE CLOSED DOOR THAT WE DO NOT SEE THE ONE THAT HAS OPENED FOR US...BY ALEXANDER GRAHAM BELL. IN THE BLINK OF AN EYE EVERYTHING CAN CHANGE. SO FORGIVE OFTEN AND LOVE WITH ALL YOUR HEART. YOU MAY NOT HAVE THAT CHANCE AGAIN...BY ZIG ZIGLAR.

GIVE YOURSELF A CHANCE TO HEAL. GIVE YOURSELF TIME. GIVE UP THE THINGS YOU NEED TO, SO THAT YOU CAN MAKE TIME FOR YOUR HEALING. YOU WON'T REGRET IT. PROMISE...BY BUTTERFLIES&PEBBLES. THE HARDER YOU TRY TO FORGET SOMETHING, THE MORE YOU THINK ABOUT IT UNCONSCIOUSLY, RELAX, BREATHE AND RELEASE...UNKNOWN. GO OUT AND SEIZE THE BEAUTY AND THE WONDER OF THIS DAY!...BY INCREDIBLE JOY. CHOOSE TO BE HAPPY, CHOOSE TO LOOK ON THE BRIGHT SIDE...BY JOEL OSTEEN. THIS WEEK IT IS AIMLESSNESS AND DISTRACTION OR IT IS AMBITION AND DISCIPLINE. WE ALONE CHOOSE WHICH WILL WIN....BY BRENDON BURCHARD.

STOP WASTING YOUR TIME WITH REGRET. TIME SPENT WITH REGRET MAY OCCUPY YOUR MIND, BUT REGRET IS NO FRIEND OF YOURS!...BY ZEN-SATIONAL LIVING. IF YOU REALISE HOW POWERFUL YOUR THOUGHTS ARE, YOU WOULD NEVER THINK A NEGATIVE THOUGHT...BY PEACE PILGRIM. YOU HAVE THE POWER TO TAKE AWAY SOMEONE'S HAPPINESS BY REFUSING TO FORGIVE. THAT SOMEONE IS YOU...BY ALAN COHEN. I FORGIVE MYSELF, AND THEN I MOVE ON. YOU CAN SIT THERE FOREVER, LAMENTING ABOUT HOW BAD YOU'VE BEEN FEELING GUILTY UNTIL YOU DIE, AND NOT ONE TINY SLICE OF THAT GUILT WILL DO ANYTHING TO CHANGE A SINGLE THING IN THE PAST...BY WAYNE DYER.

PEOPLE WHO HAVE HAD LITTLE SELF-REFLECTION LIVE LIFE IN A HUGE REALITY BIND-SPOT...BY BRYANT MCGILL. PASS IT ON; HAVE YOU HAD A KINDNESS SHOWN? PASS IT ON; IT WAS NOT GIVEN FOR

THEE ALONE, PASS IT ON; LET IT TRAVEL DOWN THE YEARS TILL IN HEAVEN THE DEED APPEARS...PASS IT ON...BY HENRY BURTON. MAKE ME STRONG IN SPIRIT; COURAGES IN ACTION, GENTLE OF HEART, LET ME ACT IN WISDOM, CONQUER MY FEAR AND DOUBT. DISCOVER MY HIDDEN GIFTS. MEET OTHERS WITH COMPASSION. BE A SOURCE OF HEALING ENERGIES. AND FACE EACH DAY WITH HOPE AND JOY...UNKNOWN.

YESTERDAY ENDED LAST NIGHT. TODAY IS A BRAND NEW DAY AND IT'S YOURS...BY ZIG ZIGLAR. DON'T WORRY THAT YOUR LIFE IS TURNING UPSIDE DOWN. HOW DO YOU KNOW THAT THE SIDE YOU ARE USED TO IS BETTER THAN THE ONE TO COME?...BY BUTTERFLIES&PEBBLES. IF YOU MUST LOOK BACK, DO SO FORGIVINGLY. IF YOU MUST LOOK FORWARD, DO SO PRAYERFULLY. HOWEVER, THE WISEST THING YOU CAN DO IS TO BE PRESENT IN THE PRESENT GRATEFULLY....BY MAYA ANGELOU.


YESTERDAY ENDED LAST NIGHT. TODAY IS A BRAND NEW DAY AND IT'S YOURS...BY ZIG ZIGLAR. DON'T WORRY THAT YOUR LIFE IS TURNING UPSIDE DOWN. HOW DO YOU KNOW THAT THE SIDE YOU ARE USED TO IS BETTER THAN THE ONE TO COME?...BY BUTTERFLIES&PEBBLES. GO AT YOUR OWN PACE, DO YOUR VERY BEST, THEN RELEASE ALL YOUR WORRIES. HAVE FAITH THAT WHAT IS MEANT TO BE WILL BE...BY MYSTIC SOUNDS.

FEELING STUCK? THEN IT'S TIME TO CHANGE, STOP MAKING EXCUSES AND MAKE THE DECISION TO CHANGE. LET TODAY BE A FRESH NEW START...BY LYNDA FIELDS. DO WHAT YOU LOVE, LOVE WHAT YOU DO. IF YOU DON'T HAVE A PLAN FOR YOUR LIFE, SOMEONE WILL HAVE ONE FOR YOU!...BY BOB BEAUDINE. THE BEST WAY TO PREDICT THE FUTURE IS TO CREATE IT...BY BAISDEN LIVE.

MAY YOU HAVE THE COURAGE TO FOLLOW YOUR HEART AND LIVE LIFE AS A FREE SPIRIT, GUIDED BY YOUR TRUTH...BY FREE SPIRIT MINDFULWISHES. WHATEVER YOU DECIDE TO DO, MAKE SURE IT MAKES YOU HAPPY...BY PAULO COELHLO. FAITH IS NOT KNOWING WHAT THE FUTURE HOLDS, BUT KNOWING WHO HOLDS THE FUTURE...BY CROSSWALK. REMEMBER THAT SOMETIMES NOT GETTING WHAT YOU WANT IS A WONDERFUL STROKE OF LUCK...BY THE DALAI LAMA. I FORGIVE MYSELF AND THEN I MOVE ON. YOU CAN SIT THERE FOREVER LAMENTING ABOUT HOW BAD YOU'VE BEEN FEELING GUILTY UNTIL YOU DIE, AND NOT ONE THIN SLICE OF THAT GUILT WILL DO ANYTHING TO CHANGE A SINGLE THING IN THE PAST...BY WAYNE DYER.

IF YOU LET GO A LITTLE YOU WILL HAVE A LITTLE HAPPINESS. IF YOU LET GO A LOT YOU WILL HAVE A LOT OF HAPPINESS. IF YOU LET GO COMPLETELY YOU WILL BE FREE...BY AJAHN CHAH. IF YOU WISH TO EXPERIENCE PEACE, PROVIDE PEACE FOR ANOTHER...BY TENZIN GYALSO. YOU CAN HAVE RESULTS OR EXCUSES NOT BOTH...BY ZIG ZIGLAR. LIFE'S CHALLENGES CAN EITHER MAKE YOU OR BREAK YOU...LET THEM MAKE YOU...BY BILLY COX. TODAY, LET PEACE SETTLE THE QUESTION IN YOUR MIND...BY VICTORIA OSTEEN. HEALING DOESN'T BEGIN UNTIL YOU HAVE THE TRUTH...BY DR PHIL. FAITH AND PRAYER ARE THE VITAMINS OF THE SOUL; MAN CANNOT LIVE IN HEALTH WITHOUT THEM...BY MAHALIA JACKSON. AMIDST THE SWIRLING TIDES OF FRUSTRATION AND OVERWHELM, THERE IS ALWAYS ENOUGH TIME TO TAKE A STEP BACK, GATHER YOUR THOUGHT AND SAY I CAN DO THIS...BY CHARLES F. GLASSMAN MD. THE TWO THINGS IN LIFE YOU ARE IN TOTAL CONTROL OVER ARE YOUR ATTITUDE AND YOUR EFFORTS...BY BILLY COX.

THERE ARE SOME PEOPLE WHO COULD HEAR YOU SPEAK A THOUSAND WORD AND STILL NOT UNDERSTAND YOU. AND THERE ARE OTHERS WHO WILL UNDERSTAND WITHOUT EVEN SPEAKING A WORD...BY MIND UNLEASHED. PAIN DOESN'T JUST AUTOMATICALLY SHOW UP IN YOUR LIFE. IT'S THE CLEAREST SIGNAL THAT YOU ARE ABOUT TO HAVE A PROFOUND AND MIRACULOUS BREAKTHROUGH...BY PROJECT-FORGIVE.COM. YOUR SUFFERING NEEDS TO BE RESPECTED. DON'T TRY TO IGNORE THE HURT, BECAUSE IT IS REAL. JUST LET THE HURT SOFTEN YOU INSTEAD OF HARDENING YOU. LET THE HURT OPEN YOU INSTEAD OF CLOSING YOU. LET THE HURT SEND YOU LOOKING FOR THOSE WHO WILL ACCEPT YOU INSTEAD OF HIDING FROM THOSE WHO REJECT YOU...BRYANT MCGILL.

YOU'RE EITHER IN, OR YOU'RE OUT. SOMETIMES IT'S THAT SIMPLE. NO MORE STORIES, NO MORE SIDESTEPPING, ESCAPE HATCHES, VEILED RETREATS. YOU'RE EITHER IN OR YOU'RE OUT...BY JEFF BROWN. WITHOUT PEACE OF HEART, YOU WILL MAKE A WRONG CHOICE; YOU WILL CHOOSE IN A HASTE; YOU WILL BE DESPERATE IN CHOOSING. EVERYTHING YOU YOU GATHERED BY DESPERATION, WHERE ARE THEY TODAY? EVERYTHING THAT WILL LAST LONG DEMANDS FOR TIME AND PREPARATION...BY T. B. JOSHUA. EVERY-THING YOU'RE GOING THROUGH IS PREPARING YOU FOR WHERE YOU'RE GOING TO...BY BILLY COX.

SOMETIMES YOU WILL NEVER KNOW THE TRUE VALUE OF A MOMENT UNTIL IT BECOMES A MEMORY...BY VINCENT HAPPY MNISI. IF YOU CREATE YOUR OWN STORM, DON'T BE SURPRISED WHEN IT RAINS...UNKNOWN. EVERYDAY IS YOUR DAY IF YOU CLAIM IT. IF YOU WAIT FOR SOMEBODY TO MAKE IT FOR YOU, YOU'RE GOING TO BE DISAPPOINTED...BY IYANLA VANZANT. THERE IS NO RUSH. THE RIGHT ANSWER, THE RIGHT OPPORTUNITY AND THE RIGHT DECISION ALWAYS COMES AT THE RIGHT TIME...BY SHAWNE DUPERON. WHO YOU ARE BEING MATTERS MORE THAN WHAT YOU ARE SAYING...BY LISA PROSEN. THERE IS DRAMA AND THERE IS PEACE. I CHOOSE

PEACE...BY KRISTINE CARLSON. ANGER IS SIGN THAT SOMETHING NEEDS TO CHANGE...BY MARK EPSTEIN. THROUGH HUMOUR, YOU CAN SOFTEN SOME OF THE WORST BLOWS THAT LIFE DELIVERS. AND ONCE YOU FIND LAUGHTER, NO MATTER HOW PAINFUL YOUR SITUATIONS MIGHT BE, YOU CAN SURVIVE IT...BY BILL COSBY.

LET US TEACH OUR CHILDREN THAT WHEN YOU LOOK BACK ON YOUR LIFE AND COUNT YOUR BLESSINGS, THESE BLESSINGS WILL NOT BE RECKONED IN TERMS OF MONEY ACCUMULATED OR STATUS ACHIEVED IN SOCIETY. INSTEAD, WHAT WILL PROVE TO BE MOST IMPORTANT ARE THE DEEDS YOU HAVE DONE FOR OTHERS...BY CHRISTA BONNET. A CLEAR VISION, BACKED BY DEFINITE PLANS GIVE YOU TREMENDOUS FEELING OF CONFIDENCE AND PERSONAL POWER...BY BRAIN TRACY.

YOU WILL NEVER SUCCEED IN ANY BUSINESS UNLESS YOU BELIEVE IN WHAT YOU ARE DOING, PERSECUTION WILL CHASE YOU OUT AND DISAPPOINTMENT WILL STOP YOU...BY T. B. JOSHUA. ONLY THE FRANTIC OF FEAR CAN HARM YOU, YOUR CALM AND CENTERED SELF KNOWS EXACTLY WHAT TO DO...BY BRYANT MCGILL. GRACE HAS QUALIFIED ME TO RECEIVE EVERYTHING I NEED!...BY THE BIBLE 2 PETER 1:3 HAVE FAITH IN YOUR JOURNEY EVERYTHING HAD TO HAPPEN EXACTLY AS IT DID TO GET YOU WHERE YOU'RE GOING NEXT...BY MANDY HALE.

WE ALL MAKE MISTAKES, HAVE STRUGGLES AND EVEN REGRET THINGS IN OUR PAST. BUT YOU ARE NOT YOUR MISTAKES, YOU ARE NOT YOUR STRUGGLES AND YOU ARE HERE NOW WITH THE POWER TO SHAPE YOUR DAY AND YOUR FUTURE...BY STEVE MARABOLI. WHEN YOU FACE YOUR FEARS YOU FIND YOUR TRUE STRENGTH. YOU WILL HAVE ACCESS TO A CLARITY THAT WAS NOT AVAILABLE TO YOU EARLIER. AS YOU RELEASE YOUR FEAR, THE GUIDANCE, ANSWERS

AND SUPPORT YOU NEED WILL SHOW UP IN A WONDERFUL AND OFTEN SURPRISING WAYS...BY SHERRI BISHOP. KNOWLEDGE IS POWER. APPLIED KNOWLEDGE IS EVEN MORE POWERFUL. WHAT ARE YOU WAITING FOR??...GET EMPOWERED...BY D. RISEBOROUGH. COMMON SENSE IS NOT A GIFT IT'S A PUNISHMENT BECAUSE YOU STILL HAVE TO DEAL WITH EVERYONE WHO DOESN'T HAVE IT...BY ROCK 103. ACCEPTANCE IS NOT SUBMISSION; IT IS ACKNOWLEDGEMENT OF THE FACT OF A SITUATION. THEN DECIDING WHAT YOU'RE GOING TO DO ABOUT IT...BY KATHLEEN CASEY THEISEN.

FORGIVING EVERYONE AND EVERYTHING, RIGHT NOW, TAKES FAITH THAT IT HAPPENED FOR A REASON AND FOR THE LESSONS THAT MAY BE YET UNKNOWN...AND THE COURAGE TO STEP OUT AND TRUST AGAIN. IT IS WORTH THE RISK TO BE FREE FROM THE WEIGHT OF THOSE MEMORIES, SO VERY WORTH IT! LET IT GO FOR THE SAKE OF YOUR SOUL...BY LISA PROSEN. DESTROY NEGATIVE THOUGHTS WHEN THEY FIRST APPEAR. THIS IS WHEN THEY'RE THE WEAKEST...BY SONGICLE MAKWA. THERE IS A NOBILITY IN COMPASSION, A BEAUTY IN EMPATHY, A GRACE IN FORGIVENESS...BY JOHN CONNOLLY. THE TRUTH IS UNLESS YOU LET GO. UNLESS YOU FORGIVE YOURSELF, UNLESS YOU FORGIVE THE SITUATION, UNLESS YOU REALISE THAT THE SITUATION IS OVER, YOU CANNOT MOVE FORWARD...BY STEVE MARABOLI.

DON'T MAKE ASSUMPTIONS. FIND THE COURAGE TO ASK QUESTIONS AND TO EXPRESS WHAT YOU REALLY WANT. COMMUNICATE WITH OTHERS AS CLEARLY AS YOU CAN TO AVOID MISUNDERSTANDINGS, SADNESS AND DRAMA. WITH JUST THIS ONE AGREEMENT, YOU CAN COMPLETELY TRANSFORM YOUR LIFE...BY DON MIGUEL RUIZ. THE HARDER YOU WORK ON YOURSELF THE MORE THE EXTERNAL THINGS YOU COULDN'T CHANGE, WILL CHANGE ON THEIR OWN...BY BRYANT MCGILL.

WHEN YOU RELEASE YOURSELF FROM THE NEED FOR APPROVAL AND CONTROL YOU CAN STOP PUNISHING YOURSELF AND OTHERS...BY BRYANT MCGILL. WE DO NOT CONTROL OVER WHAT HAPPENS TO US IN LIFE, BUT WE DO HAVE CONTROL OVER HOW WE CHOSE TO RESPOND...BY BRYANT MCGILL.

THE PEOPLE WHO WALK AWAY ARE NOT MEANT TO BE PART OF YOUR FUTURE. LET THEM GO. YOUR LIFE IS WITH THOSE WHO STAY AND THEY DESERVE ALL OF YOU...BY BRYANT MCGILL. READ THE WARNING SIGNS AND PROCEED WITH CAUTION. MANY PEOPLE END UP HEARTBROKEN BECAUSE THEY REFUSED TO READ THE SIGNS...BY TONY GASKINS. ONLY TWO THINGS CHANGE YOUR LIFE: EITHER SOMETHING NEW COMES INTO YOUR LIFE, OR SOMETHING NEW COMES FROM WITHIN...BY BRENDON BURCHARD. FOOD FOR THOUGHT...SELF HATRED IS TAUGHT. NO ONE IS BORN HATING THEMSELVES. REMEMBER YOU'RE NOT THE BAD GUY IN ALL THIS JOURNEY OF TRYING TO LOVE YOURSELF AGAIN...BY S. C. LOURIE.

THE CREATION OF A THOUSAND FOREST IS IN BUT A SINGLE SEED, ALL CREATION STEMS FROM A SINGLE SEED OF LOVE...BY SPIRIT SCIENCE. THE VOICE: THERE IS A VOICE INSIDE OF YOU THAT WHISPERS ALL DAY LONG, "I FEEL THAT THIS IS RIGHT FOR ME, I KNOW THAT THIS IS WRONG". NO TEACHER, PREACHER, PARENT, FRIEND OR WISE MAN CAN DECIDE WHAT'S RIGHT FOR YOU...JUST LISTEN TO THE VOICE THAT SPEAKS INSIDE...BY ELEPHANT JOURNALS. INSTEAD OF BEING AFRAID TO START A NEW CHAPTER IN YOUR LIFE, BE AS EXCITED AS YOU ARE WHEN READING A REALLY GOOD BOOK AND WANT TO KNOW WHAT HAPPENS NEXT...BY DOREEN VIRTURE. NO MATTER HOW YOU FEEL, GET UP DRESS, SHOW UP AND NEVER GIVE UP...BY POWER OF POSITIVITY. SOMEWHERE, SOMEONE ELSE IS HAPPY WITH LESS THAN YOU HAVE...UNKNOWN. THERE IS NOTHING WRONG WITH HAVING A BAD DAY, NOTHING WRONG WITH PUTTING YOUR JAMMIES ON AND STAYING IN. THE WORLD WILL WAIT

THE WORLD WILL NOT COMBUST BECAUSE YOU CAN'T FORCE A SMILE...BY SHARON ROONEY.

BREATHE, YOU'RE GOING TO BE OKAY. BREATHE AND REMEMBER THAT YOU'VE BEEN IN THIS PLACE BEFORE. YOU'VE BEEN THIS UNCOMFORTABLE AND ANXIOUS AND SCARED AND YOU'VE SURVIVED. BREATHE AND KNOW THAT YOU CAN SURVIVE THIS TOO. THESE FEELINGS CAN'T BREAK YOU. THEY'RE PAINFUL AND DEBILITATING, BUT YOU CAN SIT WITH THEM AND EVENTUALLY THEY WILL PASS. MAYBE NOT IMMEDIATELY, BUT SOMETIME SOON, THEY ARE GOING TO FADE AND WHEN THEY DO, YOU'LL LOOK BACK AT THIS MOMENT AND LAUGH FOR HAVING DOUBTED YOUR RESILIENCE. I KNOW IT FEELS UNBEARABLE RIGHT NOW, BUT KEEP BREATHING, AGAIN AND AGAIN. THIS WILL PASS, I PROMISE IT WILL PASS...BY DANIELL KOEPKE.

I AM FEARFUL, I AM STRONG. I MAKE MISTAKES. I LEARN. I AM LOUD. I AM QUIET. I WORRY. I PRAY. I AM WISE, I FORGET. I HAVE PATIENCE. I HAVE NONE. I AM COURAGEOUS. I AM CAUTIOUS. I PROCRASTINATE. I CREATE. I LOVE. I LIVE. I AM HUMAN...BY ANNA TAYLOR. DOING NOTHING IS THE MOST TIRESOME JOB IN THE WORLD BECAUSE YOU CAN'T QUIT AND REST...BY BISHOP. DALE C. BRONNER.

SOMETIMES THE BEST WAY TO FIGURE OUT WHO YOU ARE IS TO GET TO THAT PLACE WHERE YOU DON'T HAVE TO BE ANYTHING ELSE...UNKNOWN. YOU CANNOT CHANGE YOUR DESTINATION OVERNIGHT, BUT YOU CAN CHANGE YOUR DIRECTION OVERNIGHT...BY JIM ROHN. EACH DAY MEANS A NEW TWENTY-FOUR HOURS, EACH DAY MEANS EVERYTHING POSSIBLE AGAIN...BY VINCENT HAPPY MNISI.

DON'T BE AFRAID NOT TO FAIL. BE AFRAID NOT TO TRY...BY BAISDEN LIVE. IF YOU ARE NOT WILLING TO LEARN, NO ONE CAN HELP YOU. IF YOU ARE DETERMINED TO LEARN, NO ONE CAN STOP YOU...BY ZIG ZIGLAR. THE ONLY WAY TO MAKE SENSE OUT OF CHANGE IS TO

PLUNGE INTO IT, MOVE WITH IT, AND JOIN THE DANCE...BY ALAN WATTS.

EVENTUALLY ALL THE PIECES FALL INTO PLACE. UNTIL THEN, LAUGH AT THE CONFUSION, LIVE FOR THE MOMENT AND KNOW THAT EVERYTHING HAPPENS FOR A REASON...BY BASIDEN LIVE. TRAVEL CAN BE ONE OF THE MOST REWARDING FORMS OF INTROSPECTION...BY LAWRENCE DURRELL. WHEN YOU SEEK BEAUTY IN ALL PEOPLE AND ALL THINGS, YOU WILL NOT ONLY FIND IT; YOU WILL BECOME IT...UNKNOWN.

A GOAL WITHOUT A PLAN IS JUST A WISH...BY WORLD MINDED. IN RESPONSE TO THOSE WHO SAY STOP DREAMING AND FACE REALITY, I SAY KEEP DREAMING AND MAKE IT REALITY...BY KRISTIAN KAN. SOME OF THE MOST DIFFICULT PATHS THAT WE HAVE TO TRAVEL CAN LEAD TO SOME OF THE MOST BEAUTIFUL PLACES AND PEOPLE...BY LIVING LIFE.

ITS NOT ALWAYS EASY, SO BE STRONG, KNOW THAT THERE ARE BETTER DAY AHEAD...UNKNOWN. WHEN YOU START DOUBTING YOURSELF, REMEMBER HOW FAR YOU HAVE COME. REMEMBER EVERYTHING YOU HAVE FACED ALL THE BATTLES YOU HAVE WON AND ALL THE FEARS YOU HAVE OVERCOME...UNKNOWN.

ACCEPT YOUR PAST WITHOUT REGRET, HANDLE YOUR PRESENT WITH CONFIDENCE, AND FACE YOUR FUTURE WITHOUT FEAR...BY KENNY LATTIMORE. HAVE FAITH IN YOUR JOURNEY. EVERYTHING HAD TO HAPPEN EXACTLY AS IT DID TO GET YOU WHERE YOU'RE GOING NEXT...BY MANDY HALE. WHAT YOU DO TODAY CAN CHANGE ALL THE TOMORROWS OF YOUR LIFE...BY ZIG ZIGLAR. IT IS ESSENTIAL THAT YOU FOLLOW YOUR OWN IDEA OF PASSION, EVEN IF TO OTHERS IT LOOKS LIKE SUFFERING...BY BRYANT MCGILL.

I can change my life when I change my thinking. I am light, I am spirit. I am a wonderful capable being. And it is time for me to acknowledge that I create my own reality with my thoughts. If I want to change my reality, then it is time for me to change my mind...by Louise Hay.

Don't rush it, let the natural occur, it takes to time to build something special. No one creates a masterpiece in a day...by Tony Gaskins. The more you fight against your circumstances, the harder you'll struggle to move beyond them. Wars create wars, internally and externally. Accept your circumstances completely. Breathe into the reality of your life. Own it for what it is. Then from this place of acceptance, from the peaceful acknowledge that you can transform what is into something different and wonderful, take the necessary step to change your life...by Scott Stabile.

When you are judged harshly or rejected, you have to be strong in your heart. You have to accept that you'll never to be good enough for some people. Whether that is going to be your problem or theirs is up to you. Rejection is merely a redirections; a course correction to your destiny. You have to remember that your special life is for you, and your purpose has nothing to do with the opinions of others. When we have been hurt we often shrink and run for safety. Don't allow others to make you feel small...by Bryant McGill.

You can't always get what you want. But if you try sometimes you might find you get what you need...by Mick Jagger. If you believe in yourself and work with joy, passion and patience you can live your dreams no matter what that dream looks like it can be yours...by Bryant McGill.

EVERYTHING IN YOUR LIFE IS THERE AS A VEHICLE FOR TRANSFORMATION USE IT!...BY RAM DASS.

THE TRUTH WILL SET YOU FREE BUT FIRST IT WILL PISS YOU OFF...BY GLORIA STEFIEN. NO MATTER HOW SMALL YOU START, START SOMETHING THAT MATTERS...BY BRENDON BURCHARD. PEOPLE WITHOUT THE KNOWLEDGE OF THEIR PAST HISTORY, ORIGINS AND CULTURE IS LIKE A TREE WITHOUT ROOTS...BY MARCUS GARVEY. AN ARROW CAN BE SHOT ONLY BY PULLING IT BACKWARDS, SO WHEN LIFE IS DRAGGING YOU BACK WITH DIFFICULTIES, IT MEANS THAT IT'S GOING TO LAUNCH YOU INTO SOMETHING GREAT...UNKNOWN. EVERY-THING COMES TO YOU AT THE RIGHT MOMENT...BE PATIENT...UNKNOWN. WHEN YOU TAKE RESPONSIBILITY FOR YOURSELF AND ACTIONS. YOU DEVELOP A HUNGER TO ACCOMPLISH YOUR DREAMS...BY VINCENT HAPPY MNISI.


UNTAME YOUR HEART FREE YOUR SOUL. SING YOUR SONG FIERCE. STOP CENSORING YOUR WITHIN. DANCE YOURSELF AWAKE! SAY YES TO YOUR GUT EVERY-TIME, NO MATTER...BY S.C LOWRIE. AND ABOVE, ALL WATCH WITH GLITTERING EYES THE WHOLE WORLD AROUND YOU BECAUSE THE GREATEST SECRETS ARE ALWAYS HIDDEN IN THE MOST UNLIKELY PLACES...BY ROALD DAHL.

SOMETIMES YOUR BEST OPTIONS IS TO...JUST WING IT!...BY INCREDIBLE JOY.COM. IT'S TIME TO BREAK OUT OF YOUR SHELL AND SHOW THE WORLD WHO YOU REALLY ARE AND WHAT YOU'RE REALLY MADE OF! LIVE YOUR DREAMS!...BY HAPPINESSINYOURLIFE.COM.

TRUST IN THE LORD WITH ALL YOUR HEART, AND LEARN NOT ON YOUR OWN UNDERSTANDING; IN ALL YOUR WAYS ACKNOWLEDGE HIM AND HE SHALL DIRECT YOUR STEPS...PROVERBS 35V 6. YOU HAVE MADE SOME MISTAKES, AND YOU MAY NOT BE WHERE YOU WANT TO BE, BUT THAT HAS GOT NOTHING TO DO WITH YOUR FUTURE...BY ZIG ZIGLAR.

ACT THE WAY YOU'D LIKE TO BE AND SOON YOU'LL WILL BE THE WAY YOU'D LIKE TO ACT...BY BOB DYLAN. THE GREATEST GROWTH AND DISCOVERY OF ONESELF IS ACHIEVED DURING THE PROCESS OF WORKING TOWARDS A GOAL. NEVER GIVE UP...BY ANNA PEREIRA. THE REASON YOU CAN ACCOMPLISH SOMETHING IS BECAUSE YOU HAD IT WITHIN YOU ALREADY...BY BRYANT MCGILL. DOING YOUR BEST AT THIS MOMENT PUTS YOU IN THE BEST PLACE FOR THE NEXT MOMENT...BY OPRAH WINFREY.

THERE ARE SO MANY FANTASTIC THINGS WAITING FOR YOU TO BEHOLD. DON'T LET THE FEAR OF YESTERDAY OR TOMORROW STOP YOU FROM ENJOYING WHAT IS RIGHT IN FRONT OF YOU TODAY...BY KIM BAYNE. STARTING TODAY, I NEED TO FORGET WHAT'S GONE APPRECIATE WHAT STILL REMAINS AND LOOK FORWARD TO WHAT'S COMING NEXT...BY FAITH.COM STOP WISHING AND START DOING...BY ZIG ZIGLAR. BELIEVE IN YOUR ABILITY TO FIGURE THINGS OUT. WITH ENOUGH TIME, EFFORT AND DISCIPLINE YOU WILL LEARN AND GROW AND ACHIEVE. YOU WILL BRING YOUR ART AND MISSION AND DREAMS TO FLOURISH TRUST IN YOURSELF...BY BRENDON BURCHARD. IN ONE SECOND, EVERYTHING CAN CHANGE IN YOUR LIFE...BY LES BROWN. DARE TO BELIEVE THAT GOOD THINGS ARE POSSIBLE WHEN YOU FOLLOW YOUR HEART...BY BRYANT MCGILL. IT'S THE HEART THAT KNOWS THE PATH, THE MIND IS JUST THERE TO ORGANISE THE STEPS...BY JEFF BROWN. THERE ARE NO MISTAKES...ONLY EXPERIENCES...BY SUE KREBS. EVERYTHING ON EARTH HAS A PURPOSE, EVERY DISEASE AND HERB TO CURE IT, AND EVERY PERSON A MISSION. THIS IS THE RED-INDIAN THEORY OF EXISTENCE. THOSE WHO MOVE FORWARD WITH A HAPPY SPIRIT, WILL FIND THAT THINGS ALWAYS WORK OUT...BY GORDON B. HINCKLEY.

ALTHOUGH IT HAS IT'S UP'S AND DOWN THE WINDS OF CHANGE ALWAYS COME FOR A REASON...BY YOUR INNER SPARKLE. YOU CAN'T BE AFRAID OF CHANGE. YOU NAY FEEL VERY SECURE IN THE POND THAT YOU ARE IN, BUT IF YOU NEVER VENTURE OUT OF IT, YOU WILL NEVER KNOW THAT THERE IS SUCH A THING AS AN OCEAN, A SEA. HOLDING ONTO SOMETHING THAT IS GOOD FOR NOW, MAY BE THE VERY REASON WHY YOU DON'T HAVE SOMETHING BETTER...BY C. JOYBELL.

NO MATTER HOW MANY MISTAKES YOU MAKE OR HOW SLOW YOU PROGRESS YOU ARE STILL WAY AHEAD OF EVERYONE WHO ISN'T TRYING...WISDOM IS NOTHING MORE THAN HEALED PAIN...UNKNOWN. MAKE YOUR LIFESTYLE A LIVING TESTAMENT FOR OTHERS TO SEE AND HOPE TO LIVE LIKE YOU...OUR LIFESTYLES SHOULD BE A LIVING TESTAMENT FOR ALL TO SEE AND HOPE TO BE LIKE YOU! PSALM 121 V 8 THE LORD SHALL PRESERVE YOUR GOING OUT AND COMING IN FROM THIS TIME FORTH AND EVEN FOR EVERMORE... BY VINCENT HAPPY MNISI.

IF YOU'RE SEARCHING FOR THAT ONE PERSON THAT WILL CHANGE YOUR LIFE, TAKE A LOOK IN THE MIRROR...BY AMANDE SAGE. BEGIN DOING WHAT YOU WANT TO DO NOW. WE DON'T LIVE FOREVER...BY SUE FITZMAURICE. NO ONE IS BORN AN EXPERT, YOU MUST MAKE A CHOICE TO WORK HARD AND DEVELOP YOUR GIFTS TO THE FULLEST POTENTIAL...BY ZIG ZIGLAR. THE PAST IS YOUR LESSON, THE PRESENT IS YOUR GIFT. THE FUTURE IS YOUR MOTIVATION...LEARN FROM YESTERDAY. LIVE FOR TODAY. HOPE FOR TOMORROW...UNKNOWN. DON'T BE AFRAID TO CHANGE, YOU MAY LOSE SOMETHING GOOD BUT YOU MAY GAIN SOMETHING BETTER BY NAPTURAL. KNOWLEDGE IS KNOWING WHAT TO SAY. WISDOM IS KNOWING WHEN TO SAY IT...BY HUNGER SITE.

MY GOAL IS TO BUILD A LIFE, I DON'T NEED A VACATION FROM!...BY ROB HILL SNR. FOLLOW YOUR DREAMS, OR YOU'LL SPEND THE REST OF

YOUR LIFE WORKING FOR SOMEONE WHO DID...BASIDEN LIVE. DO NOT REGRET GROWING OLDER. IT IS A PRIVILEGE DENIED TO MANY..UNKNOWN. WE ARE NOT ALWAYS GUARANTEED PERFECT, OR EVEN EASY DAYS. IN FACT, SOME OF THE MOST OPTIMISTIC PEOPLE I KNOW HAVE DEALT WITH SOME EXTRAORDINARY CHALLENGES AND ENDURED MANY DARK DAYS. SO DON'T THINK EASY DAYS ARE ALWAYS A GOOD WAY TO JUDGE PROGRESS OR SUCCESS. GETTING UP AND OUT THE DOOR ON THOSE DIFFICULT DAYS AND TAKING A STEP FORWARD DESPITE THE CHALLENGES IS A MUCH MORE ACCURATE BAROMETER...PAULS BOYNTON..

GOOD THINGS COME TO THOSE WHO WAIT; BETTER THINGS COME TO THOSE WHO DON'T GIVE UP; AND THE BEST THINGS COME TO THOSE WHO ARE GRATEFUL FOR WHAT IS YET TO COME...UNKNOWN. YOU GOTTA KNOW WHERE YOU WANT TO GO AND HAVE A PLAN OR STRATEGY TO GET THERE. OTHERWISE YOU COULD END UP ALMOST ANYWHERE...BY BILLY COX. EVERY MUM GAVE BIRTH TO A CHILD EXPECT MY MUM, SHE GAVE BIRTH TO A LEGEND. HIGH FIVE MUM. YAH I AM A LEGEND IN THE MAKING FOR SURE THANKS MA SIS BUSISIWE ELIZABETH MNISI WITH LOADS OF LOVE FROM YOU FIRST BORN SON...BY VINCENT HAPPY MNISI.

DIRECTIONS IS SO MUCH MORE IMPORTANT THAN SPEED. MANY ARE GOING NOWHERE FAST...BY MANKIND PROJECT. A NEGATIVE THINKER SEES DIFFICULTY IN EVERY OPPORTUNITY AND POSITIVE THINKERS SEE AN OPPORTUNITY IN EVERY DIFFICULTY...BY BASIDEN LIVE. GROWING WHEN YOU ARE TRANSITIONING TO A NEW SEASON OF LIFE, THE PEOPLE AND SITUATIONS THAT NO LONGER FIT YOU WILL FALL AWAY, DON'T FIGHT THE PROCESS...BY TRINA

BECOME THE LEADER OF YOUR LIFE. LEAD YOURSELF TO WHERE YOU WANT TO BE. BREATHE LIFE BACK INTO YOUR AMBITIONS, YOUR DESIRES, YOUR GOALS, YOUR RELATIONSHIPS...BY STEVE MAROBOLLI. OUR DESTINY IS NOT WHAT'S GIVEN TO US. OUR DESTINY IS WHAT WE CHOOSE...BY MEGA MIND. YOU MUST BE WILLING TO STEP OUT INTO THE UNCERTAINTY OF THE UNKNOWN TO FIND OUT WHAT IS TRULY POSSIBLE FOR YOUR LIFE...BY BILLY COX.

SOME PEOPLE SUCCEED BECAUSE THEY ARE DESTINED TO, BUT MOST PEOPLE SUCCEED BECAUSE THEY ARE DETERMINED TO...BY HENRY VAN DYKE. REVIVE YOUR LIGHT MANIFEST YOUR DREAMS REALISE YOUR WORTH...BY BRAIN TRACY. THE BEST THINGS HAPPEN UNEXPECTEDLY...BY KENNY LATTIMORE. IT MIGHT TAKE A YEAR, IT MIGHT TAKE A DAY BUT WHAT'S MEANT TO BE WILL ALWAYS FIND ITS WAY...BY KUSHANDWIZDOM.

EVENTUALLY ALL THE PIECES FALL INTO PLACE. UNTIL THEN LAUGH AT THE CONFUSION, LIVE FOR THE MOMENT AND KNOW THAT EVERYTHING HAPPENS FOR A REASON...BY BAISDEN LIVE. THE GREATEST GROWTH AND DISCOVERY OF ONESELF IS ACHIEVED DURING, THE PROCESS OF WORKING TOWARDS A GOAL NEVER GIVE UP...BY ANNA PEREIRA. STOP WISHING AND START DOING...BY ZIG ZIGLAR. NOTHING HAPPENS I LIFE BY ACCIDENT, NOTHING OCCURS BY CHANCE. NOTHING TAKES PLACE WITHOUT PRODUCING THE OPPORTUNITY FOR REAL AND LASTING BENEFIT TO YOU. THE PERFECTION OF EVERY MOMENT MAY NOT BE APPARENT TO YOU, YET THAT WILL MAKE THE MOMENT NO LESS PERFECT...BY NEALE DONALD WALSCH. IN THE MIDDLE OF EVERY DIFFICULTY LIES OPPORTUNITY...BY ALBERT EINSTEIN.

Printed in Great Britain
by Amazon

78725227R00079